Gratitude Unlimited:

Supercharge your Life

12 Hacks for busy people like you and me

HIJAZ SALAHUDEEN

ACKNOWLEDGEMENT

First and foremost, my heartfelt gratitude goes to the Almighty, the All-Knowing, All-Powerful Source, for choosing me as an instrument to deliver this message to the world. It is through His boundless blessings that I have been able to guide you toward this wonderful, life-altering transformation. This book is His creation, I am merely the instrument.

To my Vappa, Salahudeen, who has been my pillar of strength and my ultimate icon of perfection. As a son, I must admit there have been many moments when I've fallen short of the high standards you set for me. But, Vappa, this book is my humble tribute to you—proof that your guidance and expectations have shaped me in ways I cannot fully express.

To my Umma, Nafeesa, my pillar of faith and hope. Much of the wisdom and life insights I share in this book trace back to your teachings. You taught me to look inward and seek the Almighty's guidance when life feels overwhelming. Umma, this book is my tribute to you, for showing me the light when I needed it the most.

To Yousuf Moothappa, the epitome of empathy. You were my pillar of support during my darkest times, a silent but unwavering presence of strength. Through your life, you showed me—and everyone around you—that it's possible to live an extraordinarily impactful life without seeking the spotlight or recognition. Moothappa, I am certain that I remain in your prayers, wherever you are now. This book is my humble tribute to you, a token of gratitude for the light you brought into my life when I needed it most.

To Basheer Mama, for entrusting me with the honor of being the life partner to your dearest daughter. I deeply wish we had more time together, but it felt as though you foresaw how limited our moments would be. In those brief interactions, you left a lasting impact, and your swift departure became my initiation into becoming a more responsible leader. Mama, this is my tribute to you.

To Farooq Sensei & Riyas Hakkim, the dynamic coaching duo who brought unprecedented transformation into my life. Together, you literally pushed me out of my self-imposed cage of limitations, giving me the courage and clarity to deliver this work to the world. Thank you, Sensei & Riyasikka, for the much-needed kickstart to this new beginning. Your guidance and belief in me have left an indelible mark, and for that, I will always be grateful.

To Anto Sir, whose wealth of knowledge and wisdom ignited a transformation in me I never thought possible. Your experience and the countless books you've devoured have been a beacon in my journey, sparking insights that continue to guide my path. Anto Sir, I owe you my heartfelt thanks for being a major catalyst in my life's growth.

To my dearest wife, Salva, who has stood by me through every high and low, bearing with me as I occasionally revert to being an overgrown child (a little too often, I'll admit!). You've not only been my rock but also an extraordinary mother to our three beautiful children—Fathima, Maryam, and Umar. Salva and my beloved children, this book is my tribute to you, my closest companions in this beautiful journey of life.

To my friend, Manu Melwin Joy, thank you for inspiring me to live life to its fullest and to always strive for the best. Manu, your actions and the lessons you've shown through your life have had a BIG impact on mine. You've left an indelible mark on my journey, and for that, this is for you.

To my dearest student, Nandhitha, your curiosity and thought-provoking questions about life have been a gift. Your inquisitive mind helped me gain clarity and form insights that continue to guide not just me but many others who seek solutions from me. Nandhitha, thank you for your invaluable contributions to this book.

To the many other incredible souls who have touched my life in profound ways: I am endlessly grateful. In fact, I am not content in not being able to mention all the names, I could fill an entire other book just thanking everyone who has played a role in shaping this journey. But since I've gotta stop somewhere (and the publisher probably won't approve of another 200 pages of gratitude!), know that each and every one of you has a special place in my heart. Thank you, from the depths of my being, for making this book—and my life—possible.

And finally, there is one more person I must thank—the most important person responsible for this book. That person is YOU, the Reader.

Thank you for proving that there are people in this world who strive to become better, who are willing to take steps toward transformation and growth.

Thank you for validating the purpose of this book, for showing that the words I've written will not remain idle but will take shape and come to life through your actions. It is through you that the message in this book will ripple across generations, inspiring countless others along the way.

This book is as much yours as it is mine, and for that, I am endlessly grateful.

O' My Loving Lord!

Empower me to be

the best I can be

as You intend of me.

in this life

and the one after

Hijaz Salahudeen

CONTENTS

PREFACE

In the darkest corners of my life, when depression consumed me, failures haunted my every step, and heartbreaks seemed insurmountable, I never imagined that the key to my transformation was hiding in plain sight. Gratitude—a simple word, yet a profound power that would not just change my life, but revolutionize my entire understanding of human potential.

My journey began in a moment of desperation. Struggling with personal setbacks, I found myself at a crossroads. Traditional self-help approaches had failed me. Motivational speeches rang hollow. I needed something real, something tangible. That's when I decided to dig deeper, to understand gratitude not as a fleeting emotion, but as a strategic life approach.

My first webinar on gratitude became a turning point. As I shared my experiences, something magical happened. I watched hundreds of faces light up with recognition, with hope. People from all walks of life— students, professionals, seniors—were experiencing transformations. They weren't just listening; they were understanding. And in that moment, I realized this message needed to reach far beyond a single webinar.

This book is different. While countless books speak about gratitude, they often scratch only the surface. They repeat the same platitudes without providing a concrete, actionable framework. Here, I present the "Gratitude Triad"—a comprehensive 12-point approach that anyone from 10 to 100 can implement to supercharge their life.

My credentials aren't from academic ivory towers, but from the raw, unfiltered school of life. Everything in this book, I've lived. Every strategy I've tested. Every insight, I've personally experienced. This isn't theoretical knowledge—this is a battle-tested roadmap to transformation.

What can you expect? A RE-ENERGIZED approach to life. The power to RECLAIM your happiness. THE method to REVOLUTIONIZE your personal growth. This book is your practical, no-nonsense guide to understanding and harnessing gratitude's true potential.

Who Should Read This Book?

- If you're feeling stuck
- If traditional self-help methods haven't worked for you
- If you're ready for a genuine, actionable transformation
- If you want to see life through a lens of abundance and possibility

I've designed this book with you in mind. I've poured my heart and soul into this book, and it's packed with practical hacks, thought-provoking questions, and real-life strategies—many of which I've personally devised and applied to transform my own life. Get ready to dive into a treasure trove of insights designed to inspire and empower you!

My promise is simple: by the time you finish this book, you'll have a powerful new toolkit—the only one you'll ever need—to supercharge your life! You'll find it easier to navigate life's challenges, cultivate a fresh perspective, and live with genuine gratitude every single day.

This isn't just a book.

It's a journey.
A journey I wish someone had guided me through when I needed it most.

Are you ready to transform?

Let's begin.

Don't ask what the world needs.

Ask what makes you come alive, and go do it.

Because, what the world needs

is people who have come alive.

Howard Thurman

PROLOGUE

My journey with gratitude began when I was just a kid. I vividly remember hearing a Quranic verse: "If you are grateful, then I will increase [My blessings]." Little did I know that years later, life would throw me into a whirlwind of tests to truly teach this concept—not through books or sermons, but through sharp, (literally) stomach-turning experiences.

Mark Twain famously said, "The two most important days in your life are the day you are born and the day you find out why.". During my first job as a Web Manager at a private hospital in Kochi, life decided to give me a "Welcome Gift." One fine Ramadan morning, I woke up with a stabbing pain in my stomach. Stubborn and fasting, I tried everything short of sorcery to manage it—yogasanas, warm water, and even some creative self-invented poses that were as effective as a chocolate teapot. But the pain held on like a clingy toddler.

Eventually, I had to admit defeat and admit myself to the very hospital where I worked. Until then, I had this unshakable belief that I was some kind of human Wolverine—never ill, never weak, practically bulletproof. Life, of course, loves irony. It wasn't long before I was lying in the Casualty Department, having brief occasional but intense conversations with pain, while the staff tried their best to figure out what was wrong.

Twelve hours into this unique roller-coaster ride, a nurse approached me, her tone half-apologetic, half-bemused. "Sir, everyone who came in before and after you has been discharged. But your problem… it still hasn't been solved." I replied with a weak smile, "Sister, if it were up to me, do you think I'd still be here?"

I started my hospital *adventure* with my younger brother, Jaazim. Being in his first job in a nearby town, he rushed to be my bystander. If sainthood had a category for patience with stubborn elder siblings, he'd win hands down. Picture this: a tired, sleep-deprived Jaazim trying to catch some shut-eye, only for me to call on him every time nature made an "urgent call." He'd dutifully wheel me to the restroom, and upon returning, try to nap in the wheelchair itself—a multitasking marvel, if there ever was one.

I remember watching him dozing off in that wheelchair, slumped like an overworked office chair. My heart swelled with gratitude for his uncomplaining effort. But of course, I had to throw in a dose of humor to lighten the mood: "Next time, Jaazim, remind me to book you a luxury suite—this wheelchair won't do." His tired but amused smile reminded me how love often shows up in the quiet sacrifices we make for each other.

Next morning, the diagnosis finally came: *Sigmoid Volvulus*. My large intestine had decided to play "Twister" with itself, quite literally tying itself in knots. Surgery was the only option. Fast forward, I found myself in the ICU, hooked up to machines that beeped louder than my alarm clock. I was wheeled into the operation theatre, given an anesthetic mask which plunged me into a weightless, dark nothingness. It was a strange, almost eerie void that felt like another dimension. I thought, Is this it? Have I crossed over?

For a moment, I braced myself for the fiery infernos or heavenly angels my faith had promised—angels with heavenly flowers, or, well, something involving pitchforks. Instead, I was met with…absolutely nothing. Just me and an awkward existential pause, realizing I wasn't dead. Not yet, anyway.

When I finally woke up, I wasn't greeted by celestial beings or dramatic revelations about life and death. Nope, just the sterile beep of machines and a ventilator tube unceremoniously shoved down my throat. It felt like the universe's version of, "Oops, wrong number, carry on."

The hospital room wasn't exactly the majestic setting for a life-changing epiphany, but it did offer a front-row seat to my own discomfort: tubes, wires, and the hum of machines quietly judging my vitals. It wasn't glamorous, it wasn't enlightening—it was mostly itchy, uncomfortable, and filled with a vague sense of, "What just happened?"

But the real shock came when my father walked into the room. This was a man I had always seen as strict, unyielding, and far removed from anything resembling "soft." Yet there he was, crying like a child. All he could manage was a single, trembling word: "Son…" In that moment, every misunderstanding I had about his love melted away. Gratitude filled the space where resentment once lived.

The six months that followed were what I call "The Great Recovery Adventure." Multiple surgeries, missed milestones (including my college convocation), and a lot of time to reflect. One of the more memorable moments came when I finally went back to college to collect my certificate. Kulkarni Sir, one of my professors, asked why I hadn't attended the ceremony. I explained my ordeal, adding, "Sir, my large intestine tried yoga while the rest of my body politely refused." His initial shock quickly gave way to laughter—deep, uncontrollable laughter as I narrated the incidents like a comedy movie.

That humor, as I would later learn, had a profound impact. Years later, when Kulkarni Sir called to congratulate me on the birth of my first child, he revealed something unexpected. Reflecting on how my words helped him through his own surgery, he said, "You've been an inspiration to me. If you, at your age, could go through all that with a smile, why can't I?" His words were a poignant reminder of how even a small dose of levity can ripple outward, bringing strength and hope during life's toughest moments.

This "adventure," as I like to call it, fundamentally changed my perspective. Instead of dwelling on "Why me?" or clinging to pain, I learned to welcome it, acknowledge it, and then let it pass. Gratitude became my anchor, keeping me present and teaching me to appreciate even the tiniest moments of joy.

What I've realized is this: Gratitude and humor are like a dynamic duo, a Batman-and-Robin for the soul. Gratitude helps you see the silver lining, and humor gives you the courage to walk on it, even when the winds of life try to blow you off course. Together, they create resilience—a force that helps you face life with strength, positivity, and a touch of lightheartedness.

This journey has brought me here, to you, through this book. I believe I am merely a messenger, tasked with showing you the life-changing power of gratitude. It transformed my life, and now, it's your turn to discover how it can transform yours.

INTRODUCTION

A Supercharged Life?

Think about those days when you feel alive—really alive. They're not the days when everything goes perfectly, like a choreographed rom-com montage. No, they're the days when life throws you curveballs, and you decide to swing for the fences anyway. A supercharged life isn't some mystical treasure chest guarded by dragons; it's a series of tiny decisions to find magic in the messy, glorious chaos of existence.

I'm talking about a life where you don't just survive—you throw a party for the mere act of being alive! A life where spilled coffee becomes a reason to laugh, traffic becomes a moment for an impromptu car karaoke session, and challenges morph into plot twists that make your story worth telling. Imagine waking up and instead of grumbling about your alarm, you marvel at the audacity of the sun to rise just for you. Now that's power.

Here's the kicker—it's not about perfection. Forget the Instagram-filtered version of happiness. This is about authenticity: showing up in all your quirky, beautifully flawed glory. It's about taking ordinary moments and sprinkling them with gratitude, turning a "meh" day into something you'll remember with a smile.

Remember this: life isn't happening to you; it's happening for you. Each day is a fresh invitation—to grow, to love, to make someone laugh so hard they snort. And here's the secret sauce: it all starts with gratitude. Yes, that simple act of saying, "Thank you, life, for this moment." That's how you supercharge your life.

Before you roll your eyes and think, "Oh great, another book about gratitude," pause for a moment. Seriously, just take a breath and open your heart to what's truly possible here. Because this isn't just any guide—it's a *Revelation* (cue dramatic music). Within these pages lies an understanding of gratitude that's so transformative, it could make you rethink how you've been approaching life all along.

This isn't about slapping on a fake smile and pretending everything is sunshine and rainbows. Oh no, this is about asking the big, existential question we all carry around like that one sock we can't find: "Why isn't gratitude working for me all the time?"

Spoiler alert: It's not about the universe being unfair. It's about unlocking the secret code to gratitude's full potential—and I'm about to give you the key.

So buckle up, because by the end of this book, gratitude won't just be something you "try" to feel—it'll be your superpower. And trust me, it's going to get *way* more fun than you expected.

Imagine learning to drive a car, but no one ever taught you how to change gears. You'd probably spend your days trying to get the car to move, cursing under your breath while the engine sputters and stalls, and getting frustrated at every red light. Could you truly unlock the car's full potential? Absolutely not! You'd be stuck in first gear forever, wondering why the ride is so bumpy.

Similarly, many of us have been introduced to gratitude but without the full picture—without the tools to shift its "gears" and unleash its transformative power. We've been told to "just be grateful," but no one handed us the roadmap to make gratitude actually work for us, day in and day out.

Enter this book: your very own gratitude manual.

Until now, we've only scratched the surface of what gratitude can do. This book is your ticket to the complete picture, breaking it down into actionable hacks that will empower you to create magic in your life. You won't just be practicing gratitude—you'll be mastering it. Like a seasoned driver, you'll learn to navigate life's challenges smoothly, using gratitude as your accelerator.

It's like being handed the master wizard's spellbook—you'll finally have the power to design your own magical "spells" for happiness, fulfillment, and purpose. No more stalled cars or frustration. You'll be cruising down the highway of life, with a full tank of gratitude and a GPS that knows exactly where you're going.

In these pages, you'll uncover hidden truths and timeless wisdom that will change the way you live. By the time you're done, you'll awaken a supercharged version of yourself—one that doesn't just look at challenges, but takes them on like a superhero armed with the ultimate superpower: gratitude.

This isn't just a book. It's an invitation to step into the extraordinary, to reignite your soul, and to live the life you were meant to live. So here's the deal: Your life is already pretty amazing—you just need to start seeing it that way. And that, my friend, is exactly what this book will help you do.

HOW TO USE THIS BOOK?

This book is your practical field guide to completely Supercharge your life by embracing gratitude as a transformative force. It's designed to take you step by step from understanding gratitude to living it in every aspect of your life. Here's how it's structured:

PART 1: THE BASICS OF GRATITUDE

This is your foundation—the what and the why of gratitude. If you've ever doubted its power or wondered why you should bother, this section is for you. It sets the stage for the incredible journey ahead.

PART 2: THE PRACTICE

This is where the magic truly begins. The core of the book provides a simple yet powerful actionable framework for implementing gratitude in your life. Think of gratitude as your magic wand, and this framework teaches you how to wield it effectively. Prepare to witness transformation as you tap into gratitude's life-changing power.

PART 3: GRATITUDE BLOCKERS

Every hero faces obstacles, and in your journey, these are the things that prevent gratitude from fully shining in your life. This section dives into the blockers—those pesky doubts, habits, or circumstances that dull gratitude's brilliance—and offers clear solutions to overcome them.

PART 4: GRATITUDE FOREVER

The grand finale: making gratitude a way of life. This section gives you practical tips, life hacks, and insights to fully integrate gratitude into every corner of your daily routine. It's about making gratitude second nature—your new superpower.

All along this journey, you'll find *hacks from my personal notes* (denoted by

▶▶) — unique hacks I've developed to make embracing gratitude simpler, more effective, and (most importantly) fun. These are the shortcuts and creative tweaks I use in my own life to stay grounded, energized, and aligned with gratitude's transformative power. These are like post-it notes of my hacks I would like you to read related to what you've been reading.. Consider them your treasure map to a more joyful and supercharged life!

Hacks from my personal notes

▶▶ Becoming You 2.0

What would the life of your dreams look like? More importantly, how would the ideal version of you—let's call it *You 2.0*—act, look, and carry themselves? This is the upgraded, next-level version of you, minus the bugs and glitches. The key to making this transformation a reality is to clearly define *You 2.0*. The more specific and vivid your vision, the stronger your upgrade will be.

During your "ME Time" imagine having deep soul searching

💬 Anger is NOT what you think it is

Anger is never the first emotion we feel.

It's always a reaction to something deeper—fear, hurt, or sadness.

When we think these feelings won't be understood or taken seriously, anger steps in as a way to demand attention.

I've noticed this in myself, especially with my 7-year-old son. When I

Tips from other sources

You will also find tips from other sources I had noted (denoted by ⬤).These ideas are not my own but have been carefully chosen from various sources I've encountered. I believe they are brilliant hacks that deserve a place in your toolkit. Each one has been included with the intention of enhancing your understanding and empowering you to apply gratitude in a deeper, more impactful way. These insights are like golden nuggets—practical, transformative, and ready for you to use.

Note: All the ideas and content in this book, unless otherwise cited or mentioned, are completely my own writing. I have used AI tools to assist with image generation and to proofread and correct the content I have written.

This book is designed to empower you with frameworks—cleverly structured and presented as acronyms—that are practical tools for understanding and implementing change whenever needed. These frameworks are more than just concepts; they are actionable guides that can transform your life when consistently applied. The true purpose of this book is fulfilled not just in reading but in using these tools and reaping their benefits in your day-to-day life.

To fully harness the value of the book, consider reading it multiple times. Each reading will reveal new insights and perspectives, like peeling back layers to uncover deeper truths. Taking notes or jotting down key points as you read will enhance your learning and help internalize the ideas.

As the saying goes, "A good book is not just read, but revisited." Every time you return to this book, it will serve as a mirror, reflecting your growth and offering fresh revelations aligned with your current stage of life. Dive in, engage deeply, and let this book be a constant companion on your journey of transformation.

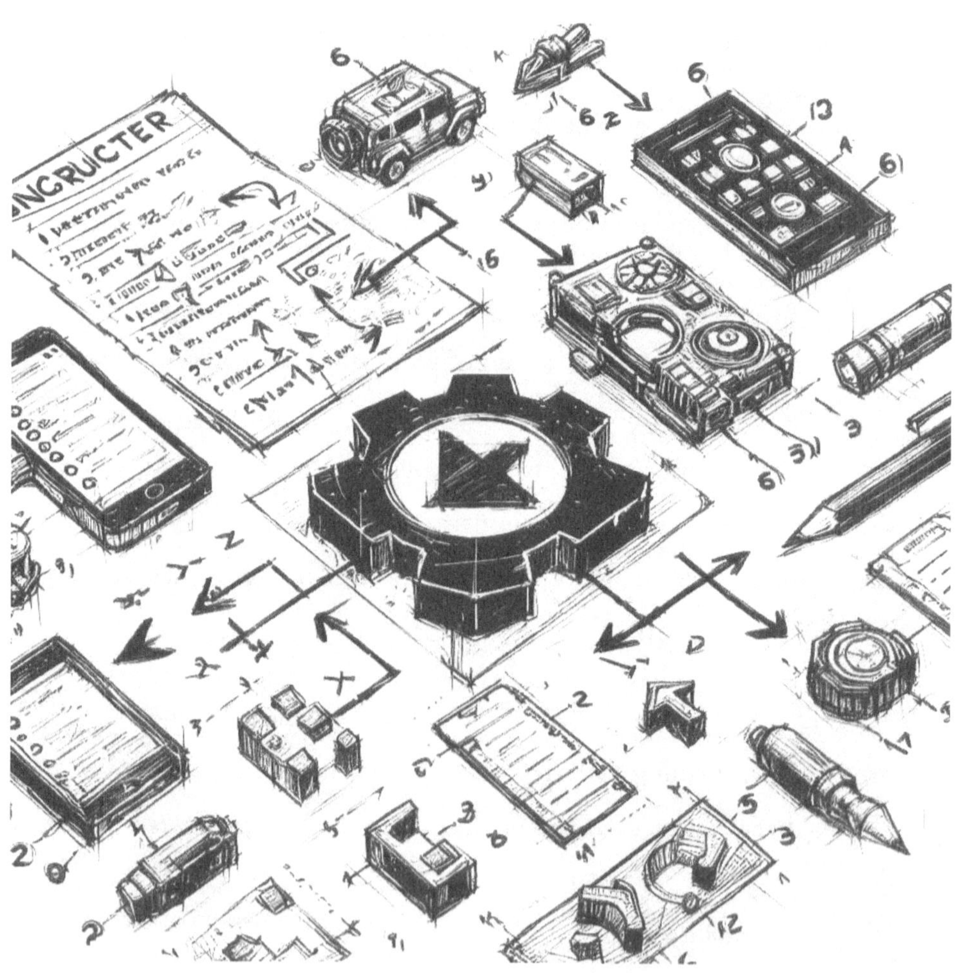

Recommended Practices to complement the book

Personal Notebook & Scribing

Get yourself a special notebook—a 200-page diary that feels personal and dear to you. This will be your *Personal Notebook*, your *Lifebook*.

Think of it this way: in school, we had separate notebooks for each subject. (And in college, I had one notebook for all 40 subjects combined!) But most of us never took notes for the most important subject—*our life*. Worse, we often neglect the Most Valuable Person (MVP) in that life: the one looking back at us in the mirror. Sure, some of us keep gratitude journals or jot down daily reflections, but I believe we're barely scratching the surface of what scribing can do.

Your *Lifebook* is your personal "settings panel," much like the control panel on your favorite app. With scribing, you can tweak, reflect on, and even redesign your life. For the uninitiated, scribing is simply a practice of connecting with yourself—exploring your thoughts, dreams, challenges, and goals on paper.

Everything in this book, including the frameworks, stemmed from my own scribing practice. It's transformative, magical even!

Note: I found *Write It Down, Make It Happen* by Henriette Anne Klauser particularly insightful in understanding the transformative power of scribing. The book beautifully highlights how the simple act of writing down your desires and intentions can help shape your reality and bring your goals to life.

How to Make Scribing Enjoyable and Effective

1. **Create a "ME Time" Routine**:
   Dedicate a time every day for uninterrupted self-reflection. This is your sacred time to meet the MVP of your life—you!

2. **Believe in the Magic**:
   Approach this time with a sense of childlike wonder. Imagine that this is the time when magic flows to the earth and anything is possible. Remember the mantra: *Write it Down, Make it Happen.*

3. **What to Write**:
   Let your imagination roam free! Here are some ideas:

   Dreams: Write about your dreams in vivid detail. The clearer the vision, the more you energize yourself to make it happen. And in some strange way you will find things happening in favour of your dreams.

   Questions: Stuck on a problem or need clarity? Write down your question as if you're asking the world's top expert for advice. Then, role-play as that expert and jot down at least 20 solutions (set a timer for 5 minutes to spark creativity). Repeat for a few days—you'll be amazed at the clarity you gain.

> **A Question empowers and an Answer disempowers.**
> The more questions we ask, the more we seek and the more energy flows to us. But, the moment we give an answer all the energy stops. (Gary Douglas, 2012)

Affirmations: These are statements you tell yourself repeatedly to let it sink in. Writing them down repeatedly is proven beneficial.

If you encounter resistance to affirmations (like "I am rich" triggering your inner critic), turn them into questions instead. For example, instead of "I am successful," try "Why am I so successful?" Your brain will instinctively search for answers rather than critique the idea, making it sink in and become a part of your belief system..

Other Inspirations: Ideas, quotes, thoughts, goals, milestones—anything goes. Your *Lifebook* is your personal treasure trove where you can explore the miracle of *you*.

Your *Lifebook* is more than just a journal; it's a playground for your imagination, a sanctuary for your soul, and a toolkit for building the life you want. Let the magic unfold as you write your way into a brighter, more fulfilling future!

▶▶ Becoming You 2.0

What would the life of your dreams look like? More importantly, how would the ideal version of you—let's call it *You 2.0*—act, look, and carry themselves? This is the upgraded, next-level version of you, minus the bugs and glitches. The key to making this transformation a reality is to clearly define *You 2.0*. The more specific and vivid your vision, the stronger your upgrade will be.

During your "ME Time," imagine having deep, soul-searching conversations with *You 2.0*. Think of it as having a chat with your personal guru, except it's you or to be more specific *You 2.0*, guiding yourself. You'll get all the best tips on how to bridge the gap between where you are and where you want to be. This isn't just imagination—it's like a brain hack for personal growth.

Throughout the day, pretend you've already upgraded to *You 2.0* and act accordingly. If your new self is the kind of person who chooses kale over chips, well, maybe today is the day you skip the fries and go for something a little greener. When your self-image shifts, taking action becomes less of a struggle and more of a seamless transition.

It's not about forcing change—it's about *being* the change. Just think of it as switching to your upgraded self, no tech support required.

▸▸ Gamify your Journey

Who says personal transformation has to feel like a root canal?

Remember the time you lost hours trying to beat a video game boss, completely immersed and oddly entertained even when you failed? Is it possible to bring the same level of engagement to something like personal transformation? Well, that's where the magic of Gamification comes in.

Gamification is the art of making boring stuff fun by turning it into a game. Think of it as sprinkling a little "game magic" onto tasks you'd otherwise avoid, like exercising, learning, or even working. It involves using game elements like points, levels, rewards, or challenges to motivate you to keep going. My introduction to this idea came from my good friend Dr. Manu Melwin Joy, a guy who lives and breathes gamification so much that I'm pretty sure he assigns points to brushing his teeth.

Here is how I apply it to my personal transformation journey:

STEP 1: CREATE YOUR HERO BACKSTORY

**THE STORIES WE TELL OURSELVES ABOUT OURSELVES SHAPE OUR LIVES.
THEY SHAPE WHO WE BELIEVE WE ARE,
AND THIS BELIEF TRANSLATES INTO WHO WE BECOME.**

JOHN ASSARAF

Every great game starts with a storyline, and so should your transformation. Write your narrative!

For me, "I'm Miracle, the Happiness Strategist, on a mission to turn every negative into pure points of power for humanity".

My Superpower? Anything and anyone that comes my way will be transformed into empowerment. It's like the ultimate superhero origin story, except instead of fighting villains, I'm turning "Mondays" into motivation. This narrative isn't just fun; it fuels my sense of purpose.

Your story could be anything: like "I'm Jane, the Relentless, defeating procrastination one checklist at a time!" **Make it EPIC—it's YOUR life.**

STEP 2: PROGRESS ▶ POINTS

The second step involves structuring habits, routines, and rituals that empower you to perform them consistently. Want to make something stick—like reading? Gamify it! Assign yourself points for completing tasks, with escalating levels of difficulty to keep it engaging and rewarding.

As an example, take Reading, the *levels of difficulty* and *points assigned* could be as follows

- Show Up (1 pt): Read 1 page.
- Easy (2 pts): Read 2 pages.
- Medium (3 pts): Read 4 pages.
- Hard (4 pts): Read 6 pages.

At the end of each day, mark your calendar with the level you achieved: an "X" for Show Up, a dot below for Easy, two dots for Medium, and so on.

Always strive to hit the "Show Up" level. Even a little effort keeps the habit alive, and who doesn't love earning points? If you manage to at least Show Up for 40 consecutive days, reward yourself with 40 bonus points—because consistency deserves to be celebrated! For any targets achieved beyond the Hard Level, assign extra points as a cherry on top.

Want to take it up a notch? Rope in a friend for a friendly competition. See who racks up the highest score by the end of the month. Whoever scores less has to treat the winner to something fun—a meal, a coffee, or maybe even that loaded fries you both promised to quit. This way, even losing comes with a side of laughter!

STEP 3: CHASE THE BIG TARGET

Picture your dream life as a massive target in the distance. Every time you perform your habit, you're stepping closer to that goal. For example, I imagine that reaching my dream life requires reading one million pages. I track every page I read and celebrate milestones along the way. At every 2,000 pages, it's party time!

Imagine your dream life as the end boss in this epic game. Every habit you complete is one step closer to taking it down. For example, I like to imagine that my dream life requires reading *one million* pages. Every page I read is a step closer to the treasure chest at the finish line. Oh, and I set milestones every 2,000 pages to celebrate. Why? because I levelled up!

STEP 4: REFRAME THE STRUGGLES

This one's my favorite. Imagine life assigns a fixed amount of struggle (X struggle points, let's say where X is a very large number) you need to endure before you can hit your goals. Every irritating situation—traffic jams, awkward conversations, spilling coffee on your white shirt—deducts from that total. That awful Zoom call? 50 struggle points down. Spicy food betrayal at dinner? Another 20 points. Instead of hating the struggle, I now think, "Sweet, I'm grinding through my quota. One step closer to the easy street!" Plus, I get to look forward to the day I hit zero struggles left—goal unlocked!

Transformation doesn't have to feel like a chore. With gamification, it can feel like the most rewarding adventure you've ever played. Now, who's ready to level up?

With gamification, transformation doesn't have to feel like a chore. You're no longer slogging through life; you're leveling up like a champion.

Remember: this isn't only about becoming a better version of you—it's about becoming the best player in the game of life. Now go earn those XP!

Book Recommendation: SuperBetter by Jane McGonigal is a fantastic book that shows you how to gamify your life to become, well… SuperBetter! It transforms personal development into a fun, engaging adventure by applying principles of game design to everyday challenges.

Saint Francis of Assisi

PART 1

THE BASICS

This section dives into the What and Why of Gratitude, offering general insights and research findings. It's like the appetizer before the main course. But if you're here for the juicy part—the practical steps to apply Gratitude—feel free to skip ahead to Part 2. No hard feelings, I promise!

What is Gratitude?

A teacher once asked her class of 8-year-olds to list the seven wonders of the world. Excited by the challenge, the children eagerly scribbled down their answers, having recently studied the topic.

However, the teacher noticed that one student, a little girl named Anna, sat quietly at the back, lost in thought. Anna was new to the school, having just transferred the day before, and the teacher assumed she was unfamiliar with the lesson.

As time ran out, the teacher began collecting the students' papers, all of which contained the same familiar answers. When she reached Anna, she gently reassured her, "It's okay if you don't know the answers. You weren't here when we covered this last week."

But Anna's reply caught the teacher off guard. "It's not that I don't know," Anna said, "There are so many wonders. I was just wondering which ones to choose."

Intrigued, the teacher glanced at Anna's paper. In her childlike handwriting, Anna had listed as The Seven Wonders of the World

1. To See
2. To Hear
3. To Feel
4. To Taste
5. To Touch

6. To Laugh
7. To Love

The teacher was taken aback by the profound wisdom in Anna's response. These, indeed, are the true wonders of the world—gifts we often overlook in our daily lives.

In the rush of our busy schedules, it's easy to overlook the simple yet extraordinary things that make life so rich. We label them as "small" or "trivial" not because they lack significance, but because we've grown so accustomed to them that we forget how wondrous they really are. It's like the Wi-Fi password—until it stops working, we have no idea how much we depend on it.

At the heart of everything we do, we all seek one thing—Happiness. Whether it's through our work, relationships, or personal pursuits, the ultimate goal behind all our efforts is to find joy and fulfillment. But the irony is, we're often so busy chasing happiness that we forget to notice the moments when it's quietly sitting right next to us—like that last piece of pizza you didn't think you wanted but instantly regretted not grabbing.

True happiness emerges when we align ourselves with a meaningful goal—one that resonates deeply and gives our life purpose. When we feel fulfilled, a profound joy takes root within us, empowering us to overcome obstacles and turn the impossible into the possible. Think of it as a life cheat code: with purpose, even the "boring" parts of life become more epic.

This inner power, born of purpose and fulfillment, is the essence of a Supercharged Life. It's a life driven by clarity, intention, and the courage to pursue what truly matters. And with this energy, not only do we transform ourselves, but we also inspire those around us to rise to their greatest potential. It's like you've become the human version of a motivational speaker—without the need for an expensive seminar ticket.

Now, what if I told you there's a 12-lane superhighway to such a life? A route where the journey to joy is smooth and effortless, and along the way, everything you desire—success, abundance, peace—finds its way to you naturally. Would you be interested in knowing about this path? Spoiler alert: It's not a subscription service, and it's way cheaper than a new car.

This road is Gratitude.

In this book, I'll share with you the secrets to mastering gratitude, so it becomes a life-transforming force in your everyday experiences. All I ask is that you read with an open mind and apply the simple yet powerful principles you'll learn. What lies ahead is Gratitude Unlimited—the key to an abundant and fulfilled life.

Gratitude isn't about forcing positivity. It's about getting real. It's about acknowledging that life can be messy and beautiful at the same time—like eating pizza and realizing halfway through that you're wearing your best shirt. It's recognizing that every single experience—the good, the tough, the in-between—has something to teach you, like those moments when you trip in public, and the universe humbles you just enough to laugh at yourself.

Gratitude is your superpower. It's how you turn ordinary days into adventures, how you find joy in the journey, and how you charge up your spirit—kind of like your morning coffee, but with fewer jitters and more heartwarming side effects.

Gratitude is the gateway. A supercharged life is your destination.

The Cambridge English Dictionary defines gratitude as "a strong feeling of appreciation to someone or something for what the person has done to help you." While this is technically correct, it only scratches the surface of what gratitude truly encompasses.

To fully grasp the depth of gratitude, let's explore how some of the greatest minds have perceived it. Wait! Why do we need to look at different perspectives of gratitude? Here's an analogy: Three blind men, curious to understand what an elephant is, each touched a different part of the animal. One touched its trunk and concluded that an elephant was like a thick snake. Another touched its leg and declared that an elephant was like a sturdy tree. The third man touched its tail and was sure the elephant resembled a rope. Each of them had part of the truth, but their limited perception kept them from seeing the whole picture.

In much the same way, our understanding of life and its miracles is often incomplete. To even begin to comprehend the immense power and possibilities of gratitude, we need to explore it from multiple angles. It's like trying to describe pizza—if you've only tasted the crust, you might think it's just bread, but we all know it's so much more!

Gratitude is the foundation of all abundance.
"Acknowledging the good that you already have in your life is the foundation for all abundance." — *Eckhart Tolle*

Gratitude is the best prayer.
"If the only prayer you said in your whole life was, 'thank you,' that would suffice." — *Meister Eckhart*

Gratitude turns denial into acceptance.
"Gratitude turns what we have into enough, and more. It turns denial into acceptance, chaos into order, confusion into clarity." — *Melody Beattie*

Gratitude transforms your entire outlook.
"Gratitude is one of the most powerful human emotions. Once

expressed, it changes attitude, brightens outlook, and broadens our perspective." — *Germany Kent*

Gratitude separates privilege from entitlement.

"What separates privilege from entitlement is gratitude." — *Brené Brown*

These quotes point to a simple truth—gratitude is much more than a fleeting emotion or a polite "thank you." It's a transformative way of living that can shift your mindset, enhance your relationships, and create lasting joy in your life.

Gratitude allows us to step back and see the bigger picture. It helps us appreciate the world not just for its individual pieces but as a magnificent, interconnected whole.

For the purpose of this book, I'd like to offer my own understanding: **Gratitude is the right way to live life**. It is not just a momentary feeling but a profound shift in how we experience everything. By choosing to live with gratitude, we unlock the beauty, abundance, and joy that already exist around us.

44

Gratitude is not only the greatest of virtues but the parent of all others.

Cicero (Roman Philosopher)

Why Gratitude?

Simon Sinek, in his bestselling book Start with Why, emphasizes the importance of beginning with a clear purpose. He explains that consistency is the key to achieving success—whether at an individual or organizational level—and that consistency is directly tied to the clarity and strength of the "Why" behind the effort. The stronger the "Why," the deeper the commitment to persevere, no matter the challenges. Kind of like trying to get out of bed when you have a solid reason—like the smell of coffee waiting for you.

I believe the reason you are reading this book is because you're searching for a way to supercharge your life. But let me ask you: Why do you want that? Deep down, all of us have an innate desire to live a life of fulfillment—a life where we discover and realize our true purpose. We yearn for a sense of meaning, for the assurance that our lives have made a difference, that we have left the world better than we found it—kind of like your house after you've cleaned it (a very rare and fulfilling moment!).

Once, someone asked, "What is the richest land on Earth?" The audience eagerly answered—the oil fields of Saudi Arabia, the diamond mines of Africa, and other such treasures. But the real answer left everyone speechless: the graveyards. (Cue the dramatic music.) You see, in graveyards lie countless untold stories, unspoken words, unshared ideas, and unrealized dreams—basically, all the things you said you would do tomorrow, but tomorrow never came. Ideas that could have changed lives—and the world. Words that, if spoken, could have made the world a far better place. And why didn't they? A lack of a strong "Why."

Only when we have a purpose powerful enough do we dare to dream—and act on those dreams. Most of us know what we should be doing to live a fulfilling life, but fear, doubt, and procrastination hold us back. We let opportunities slip by, waiting for the "right" moment, and those dreams remain as untapped potential. The truth is, if we don't start now, those ideas, like so many others, will go with us to the graveyard, unrealized.

A life without purpose, after all, is no life at all. To truly live is to embrace your purpose, fuel it with passion, and channel it into everything you do. Gratitude has the power to help you uncover your purpose and step into the best version of yourself—and this book will be your guide on that transformative journey.

To bring about any powerful and long-lasting change, we need to redefine and transform ourselves at the core level of our identity. I recall an uncle of mine who was a chain smoker, so much so that we jokingly referred to him as a "walking fire engine." He had tried countless ways to quit smoking, and everyone who loved him made their best efforts to help him.

My uncle had an only son whom he loved deeply. His son had one child—a grandson whom my uncle adored. His son lived abroad and visited my uncle during summer vacations. Concerned about the impact of his habit, my uncle didn't want his son to be affected or for his grandson to learn about his smoking. To hide his addiction, he kept his pack of cigarettes concealed in the electric meter box outside the house. Every day after lunch, he would sneak out discreetly, smoke, and return as if nothing had happened.

One day, while he sneaked out for his usual smoke, his grandson followed him unnoticed. Just as my uncle lit the cigarette and was about to take a puff, his grandson innocently asked, "Grandpa, could you also give me one?"

That innocent question shook him to his core. At that moment, my uncle realized the harmful example he was setting for his grandson. Determined to be a good role model, he experienced a profound shift in his identity. This realization helped him quit smoking abruptly—a feat he and others had struggled with for years.

You are an agent of Alchemy, destined to transmute all negativity into points of empowerment for mankind. No darkness can escape you without being transformed into light. You have the power to extract wisdom from every shadow, turn obstacles into opportunities, and transform pain into purpose.

Every struggle you encounter becomes a tool for shaping a brighter, stronger future—not just for yourself, but for others as well. Where despair once lingered, you bring hope; where fear resided, you ignite courage. This is your calling, your purpose—to take all that is dark and redefine it as a force for growth and transformation.

And the time to begin is now. Every step you take today brings you closer to unlocking the limitless potential within you, powered by gratitude. Don't let this moment slip away—your extraordinary, supercharged life is waiting. (P.S. It's not going to wait forever, though.)

Gratitude CAREs for you

Gratitude is a simple yet profound practice that has the power to transform our lives. But to truly understand its full potential, it helps to look at it through a philosophical lens. After all, everyone sees the world a bit differently—kind of like how some people think pineapple belongs on pizza, and others think it's a crime against humanity. How we interpret life's experiences deeply influences our actions and well-being. For those of you who love numbers, there's a growing body of research that proves gratitude does more than just make us feel warm and fuzzy—it also boosts our physical health and emotional well-being. While the research is vast, one thing we know for sure is that gratitude can reshape how we live—and trust me, this list of studies is just the tip of the iceberg.

To make this concept even easier to digest (because we all love a good shortcut & I have chronic Acronymania), I've come up with an acronym—C.A.R.E.—that sums up the core benefits of gratitude. (Throughout this book, I've got more of these handy frameworks to make it easier for you to embrace the full power of gratitude and live your best, most grateful life.) So, let's dive into what it really means for gratitude to "CARE" for you. (Spoiler: It's not sending you flowers and chocolates, but it's close.)

C - Connects You
A - Amplifies You
R - Rescues You
E - Enables You

C - Connects You

Gratitude connects you to the Source.

Gratitude connects you to the world and everyone in it.

We live in a world filled with wonders and miracles, but the true magic of life only reveals itself when we connect with it. This connection is twofold: first, with the Almighty or Source of all things, and second, with the world around us—the people, nature, and experiences that make up our lives.

When we express gratitude, we acknowledge that we are part of something much greater than ourselves. Imagine each person, each moment, each opportunity as a unique thread in a grand tapestry. Without you, the tapestry is incomplete. But when you disconnect from this, you lose your sense of purpose, and the weight of isolation can creep into your mind as despair or depression.

Think of Viktor Frankl, the renowned psychiatrist and Holocaust survivor. This guy didn't just survive unimaginable suffering, he also wrote a book that you should probably read immediately—"Man's Search for Meaning." Despite enduring horrors that would have made most of us give up on humanity altogether, Frankl found meaning in life by connecting to something greater than his circumstances—his belief in humanity, and in the Source of life itself. He said, "When we are no longer able to change a situation, we are challenged to change ourselves." So, the next time you're feeling like life has you in a chokehold, remember Viktor Frankl, who turned his darkest hours into a guidebook for finding purpose. Gratitude helps us find that same connection, allowing us to find purpose, even when everything around us seems bleak.

A - Amplifies You

"If you are grateful, I will surely increase you [in favor]" (Quran, 14:7).

Whether through spiritual teachings or secular philosophies, the message is the same: gratitude has the power to amplify the best parts of life. When we start living in gratitude, we shift our focus. Suddenly, what seemed trivial becomes precious, and we begin to see the abundance that surrounds us. This shift doesn't just brighten our perspective—it magnifies the goodness in our lives, helping us grow into our fullest potential.

Consider Oprah Winfrey, who has often shared how keeping a daily gratitude journal transformed her outlook. She started writing down five things she was grateful for every day, no matter how small. Yes, even things like "I'm grateful my coffee wasn't cold today!" Over time, this simple practice amplified her sense of joy, purpose, and connection, leading her to incredible personal and professional heights. Gratitude, when practiced consistently, takes you to places you never dreamed possible. And if Oprah can make gratitude work—while running an empire, hosting a show, and being generally fabulous—I'm pretty sure you can, too!

R - Rescues You

Gratitude rescues you from what stands in the way of your growth.

Even on the sunniest of days, shadows exist. In life, it's easy to lose our way or get overwhelmed by challenges. When everything around us feels dark, when our own inner light dims, it can seem impossible to move forward. The fear of the unknown or the weight of hardship can paralyze us. But gratitude works like a compass or a GPS, guiding us back to our path. It serves as a steady, glowing thread we can hold onto, offering comfort and direction. Think of it like a child gripping their parent's hand while navigating through a busy, chaotic carnival—except in this case, you're not just trying to avoid clowns, you're also dodging life's curveballs.

J.K. Rowling, the beloved author of Harry Potter, faced numerous rejections before her first book was published. She was living on welfare and struggling as a single mother, yet she never lost sight of the small blessings in her life. Gratitude allowed her to keep going, and it rescued her from the despair that could have easily taken over. Today, she is one of the world's most successful authors because she kept moving forward, guided by hope, gratitude—and probably a dash of magic!

E - Enables You

Gratitude Enables everything.

Imagine walking into a grand mansion filled with the latest gadgets and luxuries—washing machines, air-conditioning, refrigerators, even robot assistants (who, let's be honest, probably know how to make a mean cup of coffee by now). But when you try to use them, nothing works. Why? There's no electricity. All these shiny devices, despite their impressive potential, are as useful as a paperweight without the power source to make them run.

Your life is like this mansion. You've got talents, skills, experiences, and resources—all designed to help you reach your highest potential. But without gratitude, these blessings can feel more like clutter than assets. Gratitude is the electricity that powers up your gifts. It flips the switch, allowing you to tap into your capabilities and make your blessings work for you—rather than just gather dust.

Think about Nick Vujicic, born without arms or legs. Despite his limitations, Nick leads a life full of gratitude. He often shares how his gratitude allows him to view his life not as a burden, but as an opportunity. This mindset has powered him to become a motivational speaker, inspiring millions to overcome adversity through gratitude and faith. Once gratitude fuels your perspective, even the toughest challenges turn into golden opportunities for growth.

When you live a life grounded in gratitude, you become connected to the larger world, amplify the goodness within and around you, find rescue from life's darkest moments, and enable yourself to fully utilize your potential. Gratitude doesn't just change how you see the world—it changes how the world responds to you. It CAREs for you in every possible way, opening the door to a life filled with meaning, purpose, and boundless opportunities. It's like having a universal remote for life, and it's always set to "good vibes."

<u>Research Insights: Benefits of Gratitude</u>

Imagine having access to a powerful tool that could transform your mental health, enhance your relationships, and even improve your physical well-being—all without any cost. This isn't wishful thinking; it's the scientifically proven power of gratitude. Let's explore what researchers have discovered about this remarkable force for positive change.

✔ Psychological Benefits

The simple act of acknowledging life's gifts can profoundly impact your psychological well-being as proven by studies.

Picture this, by spending just a few minutes each day in gratitude, you could experience:

A Lighter Mental Load: Ground-breaking research analyzing 64 clinical trials revealed that people who practiced gratitude experienced nearly 8% reduction in anxiety and 7% decrease in depression symptoms (Jans-Beken and Wong, 2023). These aren't just statistics—they represent real people finding relief through simple gratitude practices.

A More Satisfying Life: When was the last time you paused to count your blessings? Research pioneers Emmons and McCullough (2003) discovered that people who maintain gratitude journals consistently report greater life satisfaction compared to those who focus on life's challenges or neutral events. It's like adjusting the lens through which you view your world—suddenly, everything appears brighter.

Lasting Positive Change: The beauty of gratitude lies in its enduring impact. Research at the Greater Good Science Center (Wong et al., 2018) showed that people who wrote gratitude letters experienced mental health benefits that lasted not just days, but months—up to twelve weeks after the practice. This suggests that gratitude isn't just a temporary mood boost; it's a foundation for lasting emotional well-being.

✔ Physical Health Benefits

Gratitude doesn't just lift your spirits—it actually transforms your body's functioning:

A Healthier Lifestyle: Studies published in Mindful (Smith, 2022) show that grateful people naturally gravitate toward healthier choices. High school students who practiced gratitude made better nutritional decisions and maintained healthier eating habits over time. It's as if gratitude creates a ripple effect, inspiring positive choices in other areas of life.

Restful Nights: If you're tossing and turning at night, gratitude might be your natural sleep aid. Research by Emmons and McCullough (2003) reveals that grateful individuals experience more restful sleep with fewer disruptions. Before counting sheep, try counting your blessings.

A Stronger Heart: In a remarkable discovery reported by Smith (2022), researchers found that heart failure patients who kept gratitude journals showed improved heart-rate variability. Your heart, quite literally, beats better when you're grateful.

✔ Social Benefits

Gratitude's power extends beyond individual benefits, creating waves of positive change in our relationships and communities:

Deeper Connections: Think of gratitude as a social superglue—it strengthens bonds by helping us recognize and appreciate the support we receive from others (Smith, 2022). Each "thank you" becomes a brick in building stronger relationships.

A More Compassionate World: When you practice gratitude, you're more likely to pay it forward. Studies indicate that grateful people demonstrate increased altruism and empathy (Jans-Beken and Wong, 2023; Wong et al., 2018). Your gratitude practice could be the catalyst for a chain reaction of kindness.

✔ The Chemistry of Gratitude

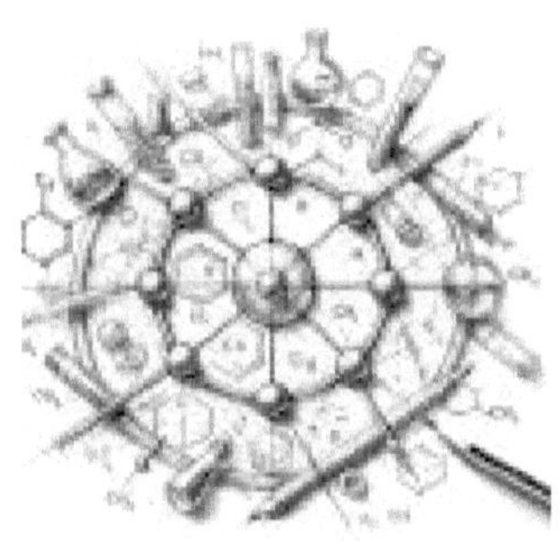

Our body's hormones have an amazing connection to feeling thankful, and dopamine is a key player in this process (Emmons & McCullough, 2003). When we express appreciation, our brain releases **Dopamine**, making us feel good and motivated. Think of it like a reward system that encourages us to keep being positive. Scientists have found that people who regularly practice gratitude experience a boost in their motivation and overall happiness.

Oxytocin, sometimes called the "cuddle hormone," gets activated when we show genuine thankfulness (Zak, 2011). It helps us feel closer to others and builds trust. Imagine gratitude as a kind of social glue that brings people together. When we express thanks or show appreciation, we're actually triggering a chemical response that makes us feel more connected and caring towards others.

Serotonin, which helps stabilize our mood, is also influenced by gratitude (Koo et al., 2008). Regular thankfulness can help increase serotonin levels, potentially helping us feel more emotionally balanced. It's like giving your brain a natural mood boost. People who practice gratitude often report feeling more positive and emotionally stable.

Cortisol, our stress hormone, actually goes down when we practice gratitude (Jackowska et al., 2015). This means that being thankful can help us manage stress more effectively. It's like having a natural stress-reduction tool that doesn't cost anything and can be used anytime. Research shows that people who regularly express gratitude tend to feel less stressed and more in control.

Endorphins, our body's natural feel-good chemicals, also respond to gratitude (Bono et al., 2013). It's similar to the good feeling you get after exercise, but you can trigger it just by being thankful. These chemicals help reduce pain and improve mood, showing that gratitude isn't just an emotional experience but a physical one too.

The amazing thing is how these hormones work together. Gratitude isn't just a nice idea – it's a powerful way to improve our mental and physical health. By choosing to be thankful, we're actually helping our body function better, feel better, and connect better with others.

The benefits of gratitude are vast, and the list provided here only scratches the surface. As research into gratitude continues to evolve, new discoveries consistently reinforce what we already know: gratitude has the power to transform lives in profound ways. A detailed exploration of every research study on this topic lies beyond the scope of this book. However, it is more than enough to affirm that gratitude is a proven path from a life spent endlessly managing worries and frustrations to one filled with purpose, joy, and resilience.

Gratitude empowers us to shift our focus from what's lacking to what's abundant, paving the way to a Supercharged Life—a life not only enriched by personal growth but also one that inspires and uplifts those around us. By embracing gratitude, you take a step toward becoming a force of positive impact in the world.

PART 2

THE PRACTICE

This section dives into the practical steps to apply Gratitude. It's the "how-to" guide that will make all that theory come alive! Before you dive in headfirst, I highly recommend reading the "How to Use this Book" section for maximum benefit. Trust me, it'll make everything a whole lot clearer —and maybe even more fun!

There are only two ways to live your life:

One is as though nothing is a miracle.

The other is as though everything is

Albert Einstein

How to "Gratitude" ?

The science is clear: gratitude isn't just a fleeting emotion or feel-good practice—it's an evidence-backed, transformative force that has the power to reshape our lives. It acts like a bridge, connecting us to a richer, healthier, and more fulfilling existence. And the beauty of it all? You can begin right now, in this very moment. Every sincere expression of gratitude is not just a gesture, but a step toward something greater—a deeper transformation of your heart and mind.

Think of gratitude as a seed, small but mighty. When nurtured through consistent practice, this seed blossoms into a life full of abundance, peace, and joy. The destination of this journey has been mapped out by scientific research, showing the undeniable benefits of gratitude on our mental, emotional, and even physical well-being. But the journey itself is yours to create. The steps you take daily, the gratitude you cultivate in your thoughts, words, and actions, will form the path toward your own personal growth.

This leads to a natural question: *How can I invite the power of gratitude fully into my life?* This is where we delve into the core of this book—the message that can open the door to a life transformed by the simple yet profound act of giving thanks.

Many of us have practiced gratitude in one form or another, perhaps expressing thanks for the good things or people in our lives. Yet, there's often a lingering feeling that gratitude has far more potential than we've been able to unlock. It's like standing at the shore of a vast ocean, aware of its power but only skimming the surface. There's a deeper current of gratitude waiting to carry us further, if only we knew how to dive in.

For a long time, I struggled to find the path to a truly fulfilling life. After much soul-searching and reflection, I discovered that the key lies in fully embracing the power of gratitude. In my pursuit of a deeper understanding, I came to a profound realization: most books on gratitude only scratch the surface, offering limited perspectives and simple practices. They rarely explore the true essence of gratitude, the transformative force it holds.

It became clear to me that only by fully understanding the phenomenon of gratitude can we unlock its incredible potential to create meaningful, even magical, change in our lives. With this newfound wisdom, I have organized my research and insights into a comprehensive and practical framework that I call the Gratitude Triad.

And the first, and greatest, beneficiary of this journey has been myself. What I now share with you as the *Gratitude Triad* is not just theory— it is a method that has been tried, tested, and deeply refined through my own personal experience. I believe that embracing this approach can lead to profound transformation, just as it has in my life.

In this book, we will dive deep into the *Gratitude Triad*—a complete framework designed to take your understanding and practice of gratitude to the next level. This Triad isn't just a set of practices; it's a lens through which you can view the world, transforming how you think, speak, and act. Each part of the Triad works in harmony to help you unlock the full potential of gratitude in your life.

As we walk through the *Gratitude Triad* together, you'll learn how to integrate gratitude into every aspect of your being. This is where gratitude transforms from a fleeting feeling to a lifestyle, a way of being that roots you in the present while opening you up to boundless possibilities.

In the chapters ahead, we will explore how gratitude can light up not just the obvious moments of joy, but also the hidden corners of our daily lives. When you embrace gratitude fully, you begin to realize that nothing is too small or too ordinary to be a source of appreciation. Every breath, every moment, every experience holds the potential for transformation.

This is the essence of the Gratitude Triad. It's not just about saying "thank you" when things go your way, but about creating a state of being where gratitude flows effortlessly through you, coloring the way you perceive the world. It's about shifting from a mindset of scarcity to one of abundance, where even the challenges in life are seen as opportunities for growth.

In the pages that follow, you'll learn not only how to recognize the many blessings already present in your life, but how to cultivate new ones. With the Gratitude Triad as your guide, you'll discover how gratitude can become the foundation upon which you build a life of fulfillment, purpose, and joy.

Gratitude is not a destination; it's a way of journeying through life. It's the compass that guides you, the light that illuminates your path, and the wind that carries you forward. As you engage with the practices and ideas in this book, I invite you to open your heart, allow gratitude to permeate your being, and watch as your life begins to transform in ways you never imagined possible.

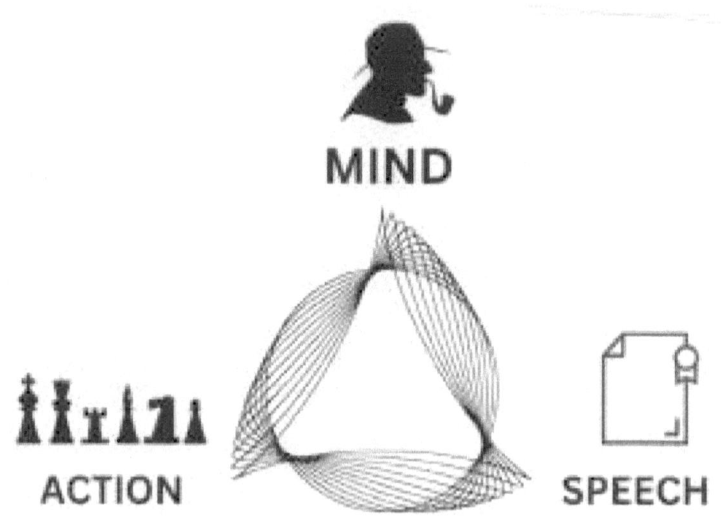

MIND
ACTION
SPEECH
THE GRATITUDE TRIAD

The Gratitude Triad: Unlocking Gratitude's Power

Picture this: you've carefully selected a present for someone special, wrapped it with love, and... it remains ungiven. The gift, though thoughtful, brings no delight to either the giver or the receiver. The same principle applies to Gratitude! If not expressed fully, its incredible benefits remain locked, unable to transform your life. This is the core principle behind the Gratitude Triad.

Just as we express ourselves in three powerful modes, Gratitude also demands a triple-layered expression to unleash its Life-Changing Effects:

1. **Gratitude in Mind: The Inner Sherlock Holmes**
2. **Gratitude in Speech: The Magic of the A4 Paper**
3. **Gratitude in Action: The Strategy of CHESS**

An incomplete expression of gratitude will only limit its transformative power. When gratitude is confined to the mind alone, its thoughts remain hidden, and its impact is muted. When expressed only in words, gratitude can seem hollow, lacking the depth and sincerity that action brings. And when practiced only through action, without mindful intention, it risks becoming a mere routine rather than a meaningful expression. True transformation happens when gratitude is fully expressed in mind, speech, and action, all working in harmony to unlock its full potential for change.

Are you ready to supercharge your life with the transformative power of the Gratitude Triad? Unlock the Power Within! The Gratitude Triad is revealed in the upcoming chapters! Discover each element in a memorably easy, practically simple, yet transformatively powerful way! Each one holds a deep meaning and a higher purpose. Dive in, apply it step-by-step to your life, and get ready to reap its life-changing benefits!

★ Gratitude in Mind ▶ The Inner Sherlock Holmes

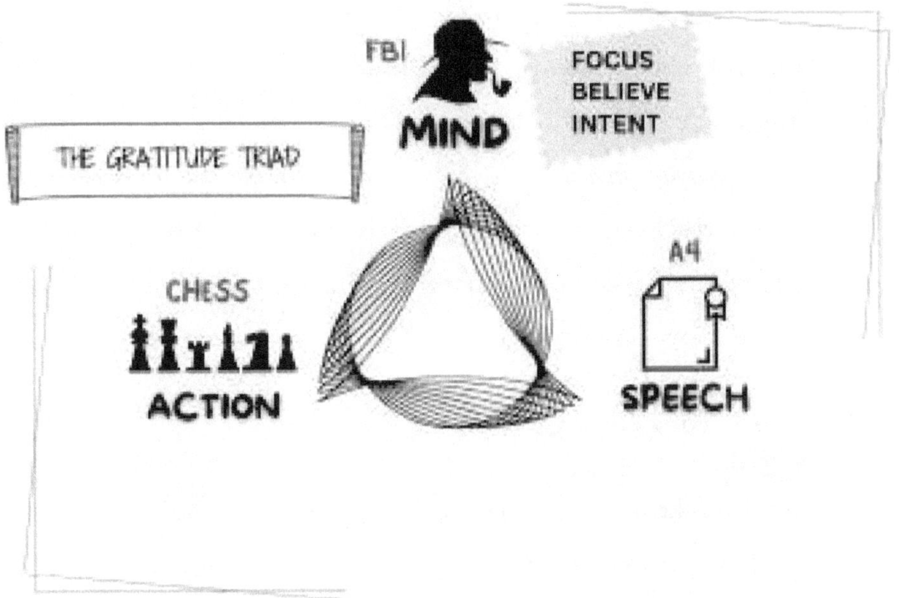

The quality of our thoughts determines the quality of our lives. As Henry Ford famously said, *"Whether you think you can, or you think you can't, you're right."* Your mindset—what you choose to believe and focus on—has a powerful impact on shaping your reality.

Consider the life of Nelson Mandela, imprisoned for 27 years. Despite the unimaginable hardships, Mandela maintained a mindset of forgiveness, hope, and purpose. Instead of letting bitterness consume him, he famously said, *"Resentment is like drinking poison and then hoping it will kill your enemies."* He chose thoughts that uplifted and empowered him, not those that kept him stuck in pain. His thoughts during those dark years determined his life after prison—a life that ultimately transformed an entire nation.

Similarly, psychiatrist Viktor Frankl, who survived the horrors of Nazi concentration camps, said: *"Everything can be taken from a man but one thing: the last of human freedoms—to choose one's thoughts in any given set of circumstances, to choose one's own way."* Even in the darkest situations, we always have the freedom to choose our thoughts, and with that choice, we can rise above any situation.

The Mind: Your Over-Caffeinated Assistant

The mind is like a hyperactive personal assistant who's had way too much coffee—it's constantly busy, buzzing with thoughts, ideas, and plans. When given a clear and meaningful mission, it operates like a laser-focused powerhouse, tackling tasks with efficiency and purpose. But if left idle or without direction? Oh boy, things get wild. Enter the "monkey mind," a chaotic jumble of random thoughts, hopping from one worry to another like a kid bouncing off walls after a sugar rush.

If we want to live inspired and supercharged lives, we need to keep our minds engaged with purpose and focus. Otherwise, they might spiral into less-than-productive territory—like debating whether pineapple belongs on pizza, reorganizing imaginary sock drawers, or planning next year's vacation down to the snacks for the flight.

Everything begins with a thought. This book you're reading? Once just a thought. The device you're holding? Born from an idea. Our thoughts are the seeds from which our actions grow, shaping our realities. They have immense power, guiding us toward growth, inspiration, and joy—or into self-doubt, stagnation, and despair.

Research shows that thoughts can even influence the physical environment around us, revealing the profound interconnectedness between what's in our minds and what manifests in our world. When we align our thoughts with gratitude and positivity, we unlock incredible potential for change.

The Monkey Mind: A Numbers Game

Let's talk numbers. It's said that the average person thinks about 60,000 thoughts per day. Now, here's the kicker: 95% of these thoughts are recycled from the day before, and 85% of them are negative! That's like rerunning yesterday's depressing soap opera while wondering why you're still in a funk.

This mental cycle drains energy and keeps us stuck. Consider this: the brain, this magnificent supercomputer, consumes 20% of the body's energy. Yet most of us use it to run repetitive loops of unhelpful self-talk: "I can't," "I'm not enough," "This won't work." Imagine powering the world's fastest computer to endlessly calculate... how to procrastinate.

But what if we flipped the script?

What if we trained our minds to fuel our potential instead of running on fear and doubt? Gratitude, positivity, and focused thought can retrain this over-caffeinated assistant of ours to support our goals and dreams rather than sabotaging them. That's where the **FBI Approach** comes in.

The F.B.I Approach to Grateful Mind

To effectively bring gratitude into your mental space, you need a simple but transformative tool. The FBI approach helps you take control of your mind and direct it toward positivity and growth.

Focus   **Believe**   **Intent**

F - FOCUS on Points of Power

No matter what the situation, who you meet, or what challenges arise, focus only on what empowers you—what gives you strength and energizes you to move forward. This simple shift in focus can change everything.

Oprah Winfrey grew up in poverty and endured numerous hardships, including abuse and discrimination. But instead of focusing on what went wrong in her life, she chose to focus on her inner power. She believed she had the ability to create a better future, and that belief became her reality. Oprah famously said, *"Turn your wounds into wisdom."* She didn't let her painful past define her; instead, she used it as fuel to become the powerful, influential woman she is today.

This idea is captured in the equation $E + R = O$, where E stands for Event, R stands for Response, and O stands for Outcome. While you can't control events, you can always control how you respond to them. If you *react* impulsively—letting emotions dictate your actions—you often end up with regret and more problems to react to. But if you *respond* mindfully, with thoughtful consideration, you master the outcome. The difference between *reaction* (emotional and automatic) and *response* (deliberate and thoughtful) is profound. One leads to more frustration, while the latter paves the way for peace and progress.

B - BELIEVE that Everything Happens for Your Growth

The next step is to cultivate the belief that everything happening around you, even the challenges and setbacks, is happening *for* you—not *to* you. Believe that every event, no matter how trivial or overwhelming, is part of a larger plan to help you grow and evolve.

Life is like a game of connecting the dots. You may want to go up, but the next dot takes you down. Just when you think you're stuck, the next dot brings you up again. This journey may not make sense at the moment, but as Steve Jobs said, *"You can't connect the dots looking forward; you can only connect them looking backwards. So you have to trust that the dots will somehow connect in your future."*

Take Jobs' own life as an example. After being fired from the company he founded Pixar when he could have given up. But instead, he believed that this setback was a stepping stone to something greater.

Looking back, it was clear that this "failure" gave him the space to create some of his best work and return to Apple stronger than ever.

Similarly, believe that every setback in your life is a setup for a comeback. The Creator has a grand plan for you, even when you can't see it. What may feel like a hardship now is often a blessing in disguise. The fact is, the Creator knows the incredible potential He has placed within you. But sometimes, we limit ourselves, living in a self-imposed cage of doubt and fear. The Creator, like a loving parent, may give us temporary challenges to wake us up and push us toward the greatness we were meant for.

I - INTENT for the Good of All

The concept of *Vasudhaiva Kutumbakam*, meaning "The World Is One Family," reminds us that we are all interconnected. When we realize this, the idea of "me" and "you" dissolves, leaving only the collective "we." With this mindset, it becomes easier to set intentions for the good of everyone, not just ourselves.

Think of Mother Teresa, who lived her life with the intention of serving others. She once said, *"Not all of us can do great things. But we can do small things with great love."* Her simple, yet profound, intention to help those in need made an enormous impact on the world. She didn't seek personal gain—her intent was for the good of all, and that pure intention created ripples of compassion and change worldwide.

Intent is directed thought, and its power extends beyond the physical realm. We are spiritual beings having a human experience, and our communication and intentions operate on multiple levels. Others can often sense our true intentions, even if they're not explicitly stated. When you act from a place of genuine goodwill, that intention is felt, and the universe responds in kind.

The Deeper Meaning of FBI

⟐ Your Inner Sherlock Holmes ⟐

What comes to mind when you hear "FBI"? Probably agents in dark suits, solving mysteries with razor-sharp focus and tech gadgets. Now imagine using that same sleuthing brilliance—minus the gadgets, sadly—to uncover and master the mysteries of your own mindset. You're the Sherlock Holmes of your mental world, ready to outwit negativity and crack the case of a wandering mind. Here's how you can channel 13 of Sherlock's crime-solving superpowers to gain control over your thoughts:

1. **Exceptional Powers of Observation**

    Your mind is like a mental crime scene. Be *hyper-aware* of what you're feeding it! Notice the negative thoughts trying to sneak in like criminals in a crowd. You need to catch them red-handed before they leave too many footprints. Are you doomscrolling or binge-watching gloomy news? Time to clean up that mental evidence!

2. **Logical Deduction and Inductive Reasoning**

    When a thought enters, treat it like Holmes would a clue. Ask yourself: *Where did this thought come from? Is it based on evidence, or am I just jumping to conclusions?* Deduce whether it's worth keeping, or if it's guilty of messing with your peace of mind. A stray "I'm not good enough" thought? Highly illogical—case closed.

3. Keen Intellect

Holmes reads up on all sorts of things—*you* should be selective too. Feed your mind with useful, uplifting content. If your brain is a library, don't fill it with trashy novels of self-doubt! Instead, stack those shelves with wisdom, creativity, and feel-good vibes.

4. Attention to Detail

You have to be as meticulous with your thoughts as Holmes is with clues. Did you just have a small victory, but your brain skipped over it like it's no big deal? Not so fast! Celebrate it— this detail matters. After all, if Holmes can solve a case by noticing dust on a shoe, you can notice when you did something right!

5. Brilliant Disguise and Role-playing Skills

When anxiety or doubt pops up, it's time to play a little mind trick. Disguise yourself as *the confident, fearless version of you.* Put on the mental outfit of someone who *already has it together.* Soon enough, you'll start acting the part. Sometimes, fake it 'til you make it work like a charm.

6. Cold Rationality and Emotional Detachment

When your thoughts spiral, Holmes up! Look at them like *facts*, not feelings. That small problem you're blowing up into a catastrophe? Try looking at it like you're solving a case—take out the drama. If emotions were suspects, you'd calmly interrogate them: "Are you helpful, or are you just causing chaos?"

7. Persistence and Tenacity

Holmes doesn't quit on a case, and neither should you on your mindset. It's a long-term investigation. Bad thoughts will try to sneak in multiple times (they're slippery like Moriarty), but stay persistent! Keep batting them away like a detective swatting away baseless theories.

8. Eccentricity and Nonconformity

Don't worry if your approach to mental health seems a little weird. Holmes has his quirks—so can you! Whether it's talking to yourself, meditating upside down, or journaling in code, *own your weirdness*. As long as it works for you, who cares if it's a bit unconventional?

9. Scientific and Forensic Approach

When you're stuck in a rut, experiment! Holmes doesn't guess—he tests. If something's messing with your mental peace, try different strategies. Maybe positive affirmations work, maybe they don't. Maybe you need more sleep or more dance breaks. Treat your mind like a lab where you're constantly figuring out what helps you thrive.

10. Strong Moral Compass

Your mental health is also about what you stand for. Stay true to your core values. If your mind tries to trick you into taking shortcuts or compromising your integrity, let your inner Holmes step in with a firm "Not today!" A strong moral compass keeps your mindset on course even when self-doubt or negativity tries to lead you astray.

11. Intuition and Instincts

Your gut feelings are like mental Watsons—*trust them*. When something feels off, it probably is. Sometimes, you know you need a break or to cut someone negative out of your life, even without hard evidence. Trust your internal detective, because that gut instinct often cracks the toughest mental cases.

12. Knowledge of Human Psychology

Holmes knows people inside and out—*learn to know yourself.* Why do you think the way you do? Understand your triggers, patterns, and weaknesses. Once you figure out what makes your mind tick, you'll be much better at handling those curveballs life throws at you.

13. Confidence and Self-Assurance

Holmes walks into every situation with total belief in his skills. Be the same with your mind! You have the tools to overcome negativity, stress, and self-doubt. Approach life like you're the Sherlock of your own head, and you've *already solved the case*— you just haven't told the rest of the world yet.

By applying Sherlock Holmes' detective qualities to your mental well-being, you turn yourself into a mindset sleuth—capable of catching negative thoughts in the act, nurturing positive thinking, and solving the daily puzzles life throws your way, all with a *deerstalker hat and a knowing grin.* The FBI Approach—Focus, Believe, and Intent—trains your mind to embrace gratitude and turn it into a powerful tool for personal growth. You become the master of your thoughts and direct them toward creating the life you truly desire.

▸▸ How I turn off my Mind for a good night's sleep?

At the end of my day, before writing in my gratitude journal, I do a Brain Dump: I jot down whatever comes to mind—words, phrases, doodles, or even gibberish—until there's nothing left. Then I sift through it to craft my To-Do list and Goals for the next day.

This frees my mind from having to playing memory guard duty all night. It knows everything important is safely written down and stops whispering, "Don't forget this!"

Try it first thing in the morning too—your brain might surprise you with million-dollar ideas or…weird doodles.

▸▸ Expanding your Mind

The Mind, once stretched by a new idea, never returns to its original dimensions
— Ralph Waldo Emerson

Life, like abstract art, tosses us concepts—happiness, courage, resilience—that everyone sees differently. These topics cannot be concretely defined which is why there are multiple perspectives.

Each day, choose a life topic. Search for quotes on the topic, and you'll stumble upon wisdom from legends. Write the ones that amaze you in your *Personal Notebook*, think them through, and voilà — your brain gets a workout!

Each fresh perspective adds depth to your thoughts. You will be able to make more sense of the intricacies of life and maybe create actionable frameworks like I do. Plus, this is one way where you can use technology for personal growth.

💬 Anger is NOT what you think it is

Anger is never the first emotion we feel.

It's always a reaction to something deeper—fear, hurt, or sadness.

When we think these feelings won't be understood or taken seriously, anger steps in as a way to demand attention.

I've noticed this in myself, especially with my 7-year-old son. When I get angry at him, I stop and ask, What am I really feeling? Maybe I'm scared for him, hurt by something, or just sad about a situation. Then I think, Does he even know how I feel? The answer is usually no—he's just a kid.

Instead of letting anger take over, I use it as a chance to connect. I'll tell him, This upset me, and it's not your fault, but here's how I feel. Then I ask, Do you ever feel like this? Let's figure it out together. Suddenly, we're not fighting—we're two people working through a problem. He sees how I handle feelings and learns how to do the same.

The trick is simple: Say what you're really feeling. Own it.

When you name your emotions and face them, everything changes. You respond with more calm and kindness, and your relationships get stronger. Anger doesn't have to divide—it can bring people closer.

💬 When you are overwhelmed by yourself

Mahatma Gandhi says:

"I will give you a talisman. Whenever you are in doubt, or when the self becomes too much with you, apply the following test:

Recall the face of the poorest and the weakest man [woman] whom you may have seen, and ask yourself, if the step you contemplate is going to be of any use to him [her].

Will he [she] gain anything by it?
Will it restore him [her] to a control over his [her] own life and destiny?

In other words, will it lead to swaraj [freedom] for the hungry and spiritually starving millions?

Then you will find your doubts and yourself melt away."

(This is also known as *Gandhiji's Talisman*)

★ Gratitude in Speech ▶ The Magic of the A4 Paper

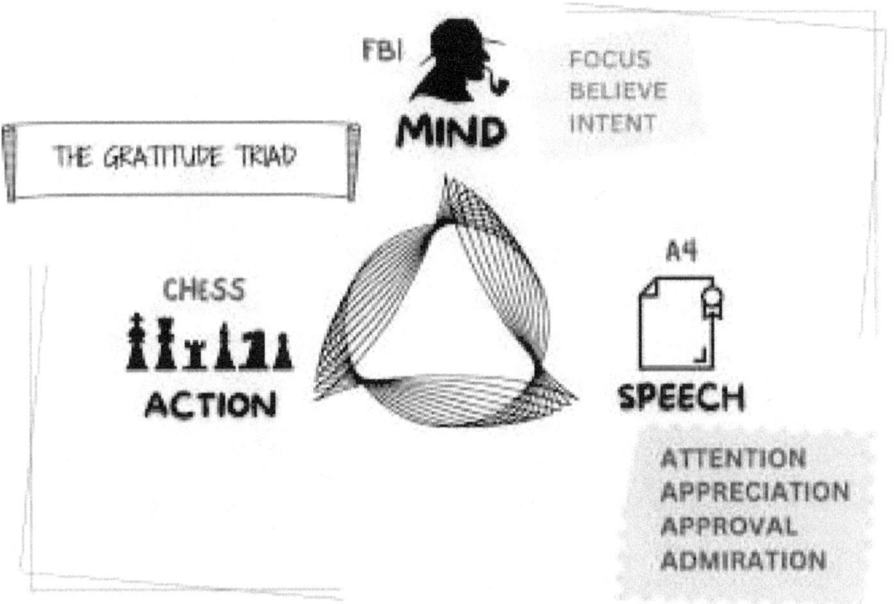

The quality of our speech—our words, tone, and language—has a direct impact on the quality of our lives. By simply making a conscious effort to "mind our language," we can create dramatic shifts in even the most challenging or ordinary circumstances. Think about it—how many times have you had a conversation that either left you feeling energized and uplifted or drained and discouraged? Words hold power, and when infused with gratitude, they can shape our reality in profound ways.

Take the story of Tony Robbins, the renowned motivational speaker and life coach, as an example. Early in his career, Robbins faced significant personal challenges and uncertainty about his future. However, he discovered that by changing his words and the way he spoke to himself, he could change his life. He famously stated, *"The only thing that's keeping you from getting what you want is the story you keep telling yourself."* Robbins teaches us that the narratives we create through our speech—both to ourselves and others—can profoundly influence our reality. By consciously choosing empowering words, we have the power to transform our circumstances and uplift those around us.

When gratitude becomes an integral part of how we communicate, the benefits ripple outward—first affecting our inner world, then extending to our relationships. Who wouldn't be drawn to someone whose words are filled with positivity, kindness, and inspiration? On the other hand, someone with a sharp tongue, no matter how skilled or well-meaning, may find themselves alienated, with few wanting to be around them.

So how do we intentionally bring gratitude into our speech? How do we become that person others are drawn to, someone who radiates positivity and creates a ripple of kindness around them? The answer lies in a simple, yet powerful, method I call the A4 Approach.

▶▶ The A4 Approach to Grateful Speech

The **A4** approach is a practical guide to infusing gratitude into every conversation and interaction. It focuses on four key elements:

Attention   Appreciation   Approval   Admiration

1. Attention

Be mindful of your words. Speak as though you would want to listen to yourself. Imagine listening to yourself speak—would you feel uplifted? Inspired? Encouraged? Or would you feel criticized and drained?

One powerful example of this comes from Mother Teresa. She famously refused to participate in *anti-war* rallies because she believed focusing on negativity, even with good intentions, would only feed more conflict. Instead, she supported *pro-peace* movements. This shift in language is subtle, but powerful. Pay attention not only to what you say but *how* you say it. Your words can either bring peace or perpetuate conflict.

Additionally, be careful of what *not* to say. Avoid the 4 vices that poison your speech: blaming, complaining, criticizing, and gossiping.

- **Blaming**: Assigning responsibility to others for your challenges.
  "You're the reason good things never come my way."
- **Complaining**: Voicing dissatisfaction, often without action to change it.
  "Why does it feel like nothing good ever happens to me?"
- **Criticizing**: Pointing out faults in others, usually in a harsh way.
  "You're lazy, and that's why nothing works out for you."
- **Gossiping**: Speaking ill of others behind their back.
  "Did you hear? Susan doesn't believe in God, and that's why she never has good luck."

These negative expressions can be subtle, creeping into everyday conversations, but they have a lasting impact on both your mindset and relationships.

2. Appreciation

The simplest and most immediate way to express gratitude is to say "Thank you."

Never underestimate the power of these two words. Jim Carrey, the famous comedian and actor, once shared a story about how he would repeatedly thank the universe for all that he had—even when he had very little. At a time when he was a struggling actor with only a few dollars in his pocket, he wrote himself a check for $10 million for "acting services rendered" and dated it for 10 years in the future. He carried that check with him every day, thanking the universe in advance for his success. Exactly 10 years later, he received a $10 million paycheck for his role in *Dumb and Dumber*. Gratitude, even in difficult times, can shape the future in ways we may never expect.

Start small—thank the barista who makes your coffee, the colleague who holds the door, the grocery store clerk who helps you pack your bags, or the friend who listens to you. Expressing appreciation isn't just about big gestures. The more frequently you say "Thank you," the more natural it will become.

You can also say "Thank you" for things that might be taken for granted. Thank your spouse or partner for doing routine chores, thank your children for trying their best, thank your co-workers for showing up every day. Even thank people for their effort when they don't succeed—like a team member who gives it their all in a project that doesn't go as planned.

Don't forget to extend your gratitude to the invisible forces that support your life. Thank the Almighty, the Universe, or whatever Higher Power you believe in, for the countless blessings that fill your life—your health, your home, the food you eat, and the people who love you. This spiritual gratitude helps remind us of the bigger picture and grounds us in humility and abundance. Each blessing is a gift, and recognizing this every day keeps us mindful of how fortunate we truly are.

3. Approval

Give your approval freely when you witness goodness around you. People thrive on acknowledgement. Think about how energized you feel when someone praises your efforts. That feeling of being seen and valued drives us to do even better. Your words of approval can have that same impact on others.

Consider the story of Thomas Edison and his mother. When Edison was a child, his teacher sent him home with a note, claiming that he was "too dumb to learn." His mother, refusing to accept this, told young Edison that the school didn't have the resources to teach him because he was so bright. This small act of approval—her belief in his potential—ignited the spark that eventually led to his invention of the lightbulb. Your words of approval can change someone's future. A simple "Good job!" or "You're doing something amazing" can be enough to inspire greatness.

4. Admiration

Admiration is about recognizing the unique brilliance in others. Be generous with your compliments, especially when they are rooted in sincerity.

A powerful example of this comes from the life of Nelson Mandela. During his imprisonment, Mandela often praised his fellow inmates, encouraging them to see their own strengths even in the darkest times. His words of admiration and respect lifted their spirits and solidified unity among them. By admiring others, Mandela fostered resilience and hope. In the same way, your admiration for others can help them see their worth and potential.

Be on the lookout for moments to express admiration. Whether it's for a skill, an accomplishment, or a person's character, let your words shine light on the greatness in others.

The Deeper Meaning of A4

✺ The Magical A4 Paper ✺

Speak as though your words could be read by the entire world.

Imagine we each wore a magical A4 sheet on our chest, where every word we spoke instantly appeared for all to read—a real-time "speech billboard." Would you still be as quick to complain about traffic or throw that snarky comment at the barista? Suddenly, every word becomes a public statement. Terrifying, isn't it?

Living with gratitude in your speech is like editing that magical paper in real time. Instead of scribbling negativity, fill it with kindness, humor, and maybe the occasional poor joke. Why? Because nobody wants to read your invisible grumbles on repeat.

Words are like toothpaste—once out, they can't go back in, so why not make them refreshing? Picture every sentence as a little pep talk, a compliment, or a witty remark that makes someone smile. Speak as if your magical billboard is being live-streamed on Times Square. Would you want to display gossip or gratitude? Criticism or charm? Choose wisely; you're basically curating your own public diary!

By keeping your words uplifting and positive, you turn that invisible paper into a source of inspiration. Who knows, your "billboard wisdom" could brighten someone's day—or at least make their morning commute less dreadful. So, next time you open your mouth, remember: your words might be magical, but they're also permanent. Let's make them worth reading.

▸▸ How I Taught Myself to Speak

Articulation, being able to convert thoughts into words, is one of the most essential skills in life. Without it, our potential risks getting lost in translation—or worse, staying bottled up inside us. I realized that to manifest my full self, I needed to articulate. And to articulate, I had to communicate. But there was one tiny hurdle: as an introvert, talking to more and more people sounded about as pleasant as skydiving without a parachute.

Adding to the drama was my job. I was a business faculty member, regularly giving lectures to a room full of 30+ students who didn't quite sign up to watch me fumble through my thoughts. The need to step up my speaking game was obvious. What wasn't obvious was how.

Cue my delightfully quirky solution: a single-person WhatsApp group. Yes, you read that right. Normally, WhatsApp groups require at least two people, but I had a workaround. I added a friend to create the group, booted them out (with love, of course), and voilà—my solo chat room, grandly titled *Power Zone*, was born.

Every morning, I'd post a big, juicy philosophical question in this *solo Whatsapp group*, the kind of question that makes you pause mid-toast. Then, I'd imagine myself asking it to the world's top expert...

The twist? During my long train commute to work, I would become THE expert. I'd practice answering the question out loud, pretending my "audience" was rapt with attention. In my mind, I wasn't just answering; I was delivering a TED Talk to an audience of

enthusiastic fans who hung on to my every word.

This routine became my personal stage for practicing speaking, minus the nerves of real-life judgment. And let me tell you, if anyone on the train caught me gesturing and talking, they probably assumed I was having a deep, existential chat with someone on the other end of the line.

The results? Game-changing. Today, I can articulate my thoughts on any subject with clarity and confidence. What's more, the life questions I answered in my Power Zone turned out to be useful not just for me, but for others too. Strangers, friends, and colleagues now approach me with their dilemmas, seeking actionable answers. And as surreal as it sounds, I'm now giving them the kind of advice I once practiced delivering to an imaginary fanbase.

This quirky experiment also gave me the ability to create actionable frameworks like the ones in this book—frameworks that, by all accounts, are making life simpler, happier, and a lot more fun for the people who try them.

So, if the thought of public speaking gives you the heebie-jeebies or you feel stuck finding your voice, give this hack a shot. Create your own Power Zone, channel your inner expert, and let your ideas flow. You might just discover, like I did, that a little make-believe can spark some real magic.

💬 How Does it Get Any Better Than This ?!

This is a magical question to be asked with a genuine sense of amazement (note the exclamation mark at the end) that can instantly flip the switch on your mood. It creates a sense of amazement and wonder, the kind of wide-eyed excitement usually reserved for kids on Christmas morning—or adults when Wi-Fi starts working again.

Even when the situation feels more "meh" than magical, repeat this mantra with enthusiasm (fake it if you must), and watch the energy shift. When you ask this question, your mind doesn't just sit there—it starts acting like a hyperactive intern, eagerly searching for all the good stuff to impress you.

The beauty of this practice is that it tricks your brain into elevating its vibe. It's like tuning into a radio station that only plays your favorite songs. Suddenly, your thoughts align with positivity and abundance, and your life starts feeling like a highlight reel instead of a blooper reel.

This shift isn't just a mental exercise; it's like flipping a universal light switch, sending out vibes so good they could power a dance floor. It's an energetic transformation that aligns you with the people, opportunities, and experiences that serve you best—kind of like the universe's way of saying, "Hey, welcome to the VIP section of life!"

(Gary Douglas, 2012)

▶▶ What to do when someone thanks you?

Have you ever found yourself in the awkward situation where someone thanked you for helping them, and you weren't quite sure how to respond?

Here's my take: we should thank the person who thanked us. Why? Because it was through them that we were given the opportunity to help. It might feel a little awkward to do so at first, but over time, this simple gesture fosters deeper gratitude and connection.

1. Express Gratitude in Return
When someone thanks you, respond by saying, "Thank you for allowing me the opportunity to help." This simple statement shifts the focus to appreciation for the experience itself. It acknowledges the interaction as a mutual exchange and reinforces the positive impact of gratitude on both sides.

2. Acknowledge Their Kindness

Say something like, "It means a lot to me that you took the time to express your thanks." This response not only shows that you value their gratitude but also highlights their thoughtfulness. It creates a warm, positive connection that encourages more acts of kindness and appreciation.

3. Reflect on the Positive Impact

Respond with, "I'm so glad I could make a difference for you." This reply emphasizes the value of what you did and highlights the positive outcome of your action. It also strengthens the bond between you and the other person, making the moment more meaningful.

4. Reinforce Their Value

A great response is, "It was my pleasure to help—you deserve it!" This reply not only accepts their gratitude but also uplifts them by reinforcing their worthiness of receiving help or support. It deepens the interaction and leaves both of you feeling positive and appreciated.

5. Redirect Gratitude to the Bigger Picture

Say, "I'm grateful that everything worked out well for you." This response places the focus on the success of the situation rather than just the action itself. It broadens the scope of gratitude and encourages a shared celebration of positive outcomes.

6. Shift the Credit to the Universe or Shared Circumstances

Instead of accepting the gratitude entirely, reflect on the bigger picture by saying, "I think we were both in the right place at the right time—it was meant to be." Or, "I feel like the universe aligned perfectly for this to happen for you!" This adds a touch of wonder to the moment, framing it as something beyond just your individual actions. It creates a sense of shared connection and harmony.

7.. Express Gratitude for the Relationship Itself

Use the opportunity to emphasize the bond between you and the person. Responses like, "Thank you for trusting me enough to let me help—it means so much to me," or "Your gratitude reminds me how much I value our connection," deepen the moment. By highlighting the importance of trust and connection, you make the interaction more personal and heartfelt.

8. Inspire Them to 'Pay It Forward'
Encourage the person to spread kindness by saying, "I'm so glad I could help—maybe you'll get the chance to do the same for someone else!" Or, "Gratitude is contagious—pass it on whenever you can!" This response not only acknowledges their thanks but inspires a ripple effect of positivity and gratitude in others.

▸▸ A Parenting Tip (also effective for Grown-ups)

We, as Humans, crave attention. If we can't get noticed by being our best selves, we might try to grab attention in less-than-ideal ways. We simply cannot be ignored, right? This is especially true for kids. They have a whole toolkit of strategies to get the attention they want, and sometimes that toolkit includes a bit of drama.

I've found, though, that the best way to encourage positive behavior in children is by acknowledging even the tiniest good deeds. It's like magic. They absolutely love being appreciated. And it's not even about throwing them a parade (though a parade never hurt anyone). It's as simple as saying, "Hey, I noticed you put your shoes away without me asking!"

Here's a fun example. I was babysitting my son, Umar, who typically avoided helping with housework. One day, I casually remarked, "Umar is the best at organizing toys. He always knows exactly where everything goes!" I made sure to say it like I was telling someone who was definitely older and wiser than Umar—like his grandma or someone with decades of life experience. Guess what? The next day, Umar was putting his toys away like it was his full-time job. I thought, "Wow, I should've become a motivational speaker for kids."

You can also take this a step further. Appreciate the qualities you want your child to develop, but do it as if those qualities are already in full swing. For instance, say something like, "Alex is such a caring child. He loves helping around the house and is always looking out for his little sister!" You could even let him "accidentally overhear" you saying this to someone you respect, like a family member or friend. When they hear praise from someone they look up to, it feels like an endorsement, and boom—they're on their way to becoming that ideal version of themselves.

The real trick? Focus on the positives and genuinely celebrate those moments. Even if it's something small, like putting their plate away or saying "please" without prompting. It's not about creating a pressure-cooker of perfection, but about making them feel seen and valued for what they're already doing right. And, hey, who doesn't like a little positive reinforcement?

This principle works wonders with adults too. I once witnessed a rather amusing scene at the college where I worked. In the office, the Vice-Principal was talking to the Administration Officer seated at the other end of the room. He raised his voice to tell the AO about how Jiji, the peon, successfully completed an errand and did a wonderful job. Now, Jiji could've been praised in a quiet corner, but no—he needed to hear it!

As the Vice-Principal spoke those words, Jiji, a man of modest height, stood a little taller—he almost seemed to grow an inch or two right before my eyes! I'm pretty sure that from then on, when the Vice-Principal calls for him, Jiji is going to be there before the VP finishes saying the last "-Ji "

It was like witnessing a superhero origin moment—Jiji, the Office Avenger, powered by praise!

★ Gratitude in Action ▶ The Strategy of CHESS

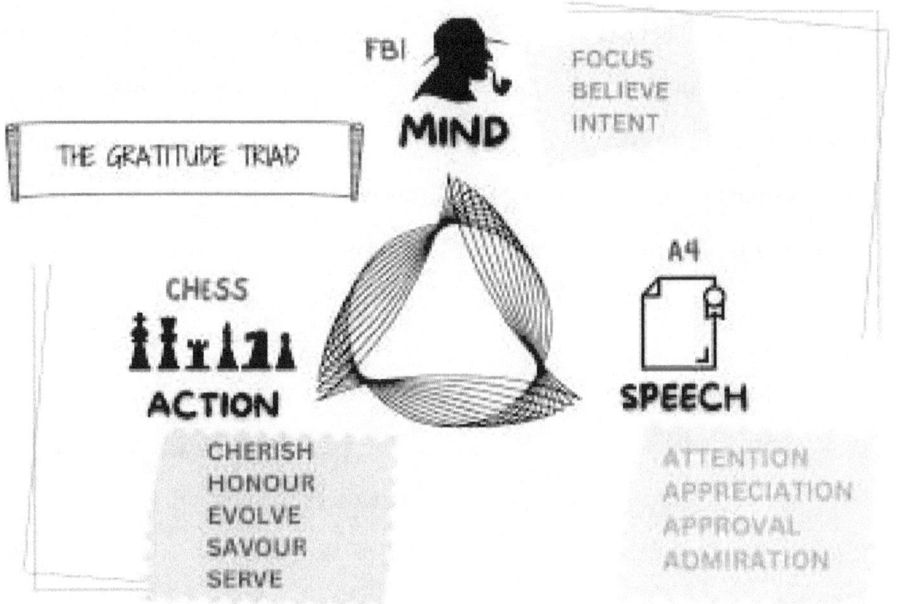

Imagine you've hired a new sales recruit for your company, offering them a sizable salary. But there's something odd about their work approach. Every day, they come to the office, sit in the middle of the room, and start proclaiming, "My boss is the best boss. My company is the best company. My colleagues are the best colleagues." From morning to evening, this is all they do—no sales calls, no client meetings—just endless praise.

Now, if it were up to you, how long would you keep this recruit? Likely no more than a few days before you decide it's time to let them go. You hired them to bring in sales, not to be a full-time proclaimer. The company needs results, not just proclamations.

As ridiculous as this scenario might sound, it mirrors what many of us do in life. We often *think* and *say* that we're grateful (hoping that somehow our verbal or mental affirmations will magically make life better), but fail to back those feelings with action. It's like expecting praise alone to improve our situation. Without backing up our gratitude with tangible actions, no magic solution will come to fix things for us. Real change happens when gratitude is integrated into how we live and act.

Take a moment to reflect on anyone you admire—a leader, a mentor, or a person who's made a difference in your life. I guarantee they live by a sense of gratitude in action.. Gratitude isn't just words for them—it's how they lead their life.

As Oprah Winfrey wisely said, *"If you're still breathing, you have a second chance."* This powerful quote from Oprah reminds us that every new day is another opportunity to take action. The way we use each moment reveals the true impact of gratitude in our lives. Many of us fall into the trap of waiting—waiting for the right time, for opportunities to magically appear, or for life to clear the obstacles in our path. But waiting leads to more waiting, and we get stuck. The key is to act *even when the road ahead is unclear.* Once you take that step, new possibilities open up in ways you couldn't have imagined.

Let me tell you a quick story about Thomas Edison. After his lab burned down in 1914, destroying years of work, his response wasn't to wallow in despair. He looked at the ruins and said, *"There is great value in disaster. All our mistakes are burned up. Thank God we can start anew."* Edison's gratitude wasn't just in words—it was in his decision to immediately begin rebuilding. Within weeks, he and his team were back to work. Edison understood that gratitude, when paired with action, creates new opportunities.

▶▶ The CHESS Approach to Grateful Action

How, then, do we put gratitude into action? The **CHESS** approach provides a practical framework to guide us.

CHERISH HONOUR EVOLVE SAVOUR SERVE

By following the CHESS approach you can bring gratitude into your daily actions. When gratitude becomes a way of life, it stops being a passive feeling and transforms into a powerful force that shapes your reality, creates opportunities, and fosters deeper connections with the people and blessings in your life.

C - CHERISH Every Blessing

Imagine gifting someone a beautiful watch, only to see them toss it aside carelessly. How would you feel? The way someone treats a gift reflects how much they value the giver. Similarly, everything we have—our health, our relationships, our skills, …—is a gift from the universe, from the Creator, from life itself. To cherish these blessings means to truly value and take care of them. When we cherish what we've been given, we show that we're not only grateful for the blessing but for the source of that blessing.

Steve Jobs, after his early successes, was ousted from Apple in 1985, the very company he co-founded. Most people would have been crushed, but Jobs used this as a time for reflection and growth. He once said, "Getting fired from Apple was the best thing that could have ever happened to me." He cherished the setback as an opportunity, and later, when he returned to Apple, he led the company to even greater heights.

H - HONOUR Your Blessings

Every blessing comes with a responsibility. It's not enough to just be grateful in thought; we must *honour* our blessings by fulfilling the duties that come with them. Honour your parents, your teachers, your friendships. Honour your health by taking care of your body. Honour your time by using it wisely. Think of each blessing as a trust given to you, and it's your duty to respect that trust.

Consider the way Mahatma Gandhi lived. He didn't just speak about peace and justice—he honoured those ideals through his actions every single day. He once said, "The best way to find yourself is to lose yourself in the service of others." Gandhi understood that gratitude and honouring blessings meant using every ounce of his energy to serve a higher purpose. By honouring the blessings you've received, you show deep respect for the life you've been given.

E - EVOLVE and Improve

Growth is the essence of life. Think about it: the difference between something alive and something dead is that the living thing grows. Gratitude, too, needs to evolve. It's not just about being thankful for what you have but about asking, "How can I improve this?" When you sit down to eat, don't just eat mindlessly—ask, "How can I make this experience better?" When you interact with someone, ask, "How can I leave this person a little better than before?". Gratitude propels us toward becoming the best version of ourselves by becoming the catalyst for personal development and transformation.

Consider Serena Williams, the tennis legend. Even at the height of her career, she never stopped evolving, constantly working to refine her game. In an interview, she said, "I really think a champion is defined not by their wins but by how they can recover when they fall." Her relentless pursuit of improvement is a perfect example of evolving in gratitude. She recognized her talent as a blessing and constantly worked to honour and evolve it.

S - SAVOUR Every Blessing

Imagine you've been lost in the desert for days, and you finally stumble upon a small pool of water. That first sip—how would it taste? Probably like the most exquisite drink you've ever had. That's what it means to savour a blessing. Every moment, every small joy, is an opportunity to be present and fully experience life's richness. Whether it's a meal, a conversation, or just a moment of quiet, savour it. When you're with loved ones, focus on them, savour time with them. Life's richness comes from fully experiencing each moment, and gratitude thrives in that awareness.

Famous chef and food writer Anthony Bourdain had a beautiful way of talking about food and travel. He didn't just consume food—he savoured every meal, understanding the stories and cultures behind it. In his travels, Bourdain often said, "Your body is not a temple, it's an amusement park. Enjoy the ride." This philosophy of savouring each moment, each bite, speaks volumes about how we should approach life with gratitude.

S - SERVE Those Less Fortunate

Finally, true gratitude expresses itself in service to others. The life you're living right now—faults, imperfections, and all—is someone else's dream. What you take for granted may be a prayer that someone has been waiting years to be answered. By serving others, especially those less fortunate, we not only express gratitude for what we have but also help others find their own blessings.. Imagine a world where everyone sought to empower those around them—what a wonderful, compassionate world it would be!

Mother Teresa exemplified this. She once said, "Not all of us can do great things. But we can do small things with great love." Her entire life was dedicated to serving others, and in doing so, she embodied gratitude in the purest form. The blessings you receive aren't just for your benefit—they're entrusted to you so that you can use them to uplift others.

The Deeper Meaning of CHESS
✷ The Strategy in CHESS ✷

Think of life like a game of chess. In chess, every move is deliberate, each one contributing to the end goal. The game requires focus, strategy, and presence. You're always looking for opportunities to improve your position, even when your opponent makes a move that seems to put you at a disadvantage. In life, much like in chess, we need to stay present and alert to the opportunities that come our way—moments where we can act with gratitude and make a positive impact.

Each move in life offers a chance to do good, to multiply our blessings, and to uplift others. The Almighty places these moments before us like the philosopher's stone—waiting for us to recognize their value and use them to transform not only our lives but the lives of those around us.

Gratitude in Action is like being a chess master, seizing each moment to make a positive impact. The more you practice the CHESS approach—Cherish, Honour, Evolve, Savour, and Serve—the more you'll find that gratitude becomes not just a feeling, but a way of life that transforms you and those around you.

▸▸ The 3 Ways of using your Blessings

The way I see my blessings is that they're a test from the Almighty: "How well do you use them, and for whom?"

My theory is that there are 3 ways of using any blessing (everything, after all, is a blessing):

DIM, FLOM, and VK.

DIM stands for Dog In the Manger. This is the "I'm not using it, and neither will you" approach. Like a miser hoarding his money, too afraid to spend it but even more unwilling to let anyone else benefit from it. A blessing turned curse—mentally, you become narrow-minded; externally, you attract thieves. With knowledge, it's the same story: Keep it to yourself and your ego gets inflated, blocking any real growth.

FLOM stands for Family, Loved Ones, and Me. Here, you use your blessings for yourself and those closest to you. This keeps the blessings flowing, as long as you don't overdo it. Sharing is key—just like passing the snacks around at a party, everyone's happy and there's plenty to go around.

VK stands for Vasudaiva Kutumbakam, or "the world is my family." This is when you use your blessings to help everyone—yes, even those people who might not be on your Christmas card list. When you do this, you'll find your blessings multiply, like magic. Share your money to help others, and it has a strange way of coming back to you—probably not in the form of a surprise inheritance, but in ways you'd never expect. Share your knowledge, and you'll gain even deeper insights in return. This is one of the reasons why most research agrees that the best way to learn something is to teach it to someone else.

This leads to a very powerful insight.:
Whatever you want in life, the secret is simple: help others achieve it, and you'll achieve it too!

If you want to be rich, the more people you help create wealth, the more wealth you'll generate for yourself. It's a powerful cycle of giving and growing.

When you guide someone else, encouraging them to take action, something magical happens—you can't help but take action yourself. By focusing on solving someone else's problem, your mind enters a state of calm and clarity. Doubts and negative voices fade away, and instead, you send yourself an empowering message: "This is possible!"

And that's the spark you need. When you help others, you build belief in your own ability to achieve what you want—whether it's wealth, success, or happiness. Start giving, start solving, and watch your dreams come alive!

So, that was the core engine behind the magical power of Gratitude. I trust that you will revisit the framework, fully absorb it, and implement it in your life. One common mistake I made initially was trying to bring about a drastic change in my life in a short span of time. No, this doesn't work because any sudden deviation from the norm is perceived by our brain as a threat and will be resisted. This is why we need to take baby steps when making a change. I call it the Watermelon Theory. If you were handed a watermelon to eat, would you try to swallow it whole, or would you break it into small, bite-sized pieces and start consuming it bit by bit without delay? I believe you'd choose the latter.

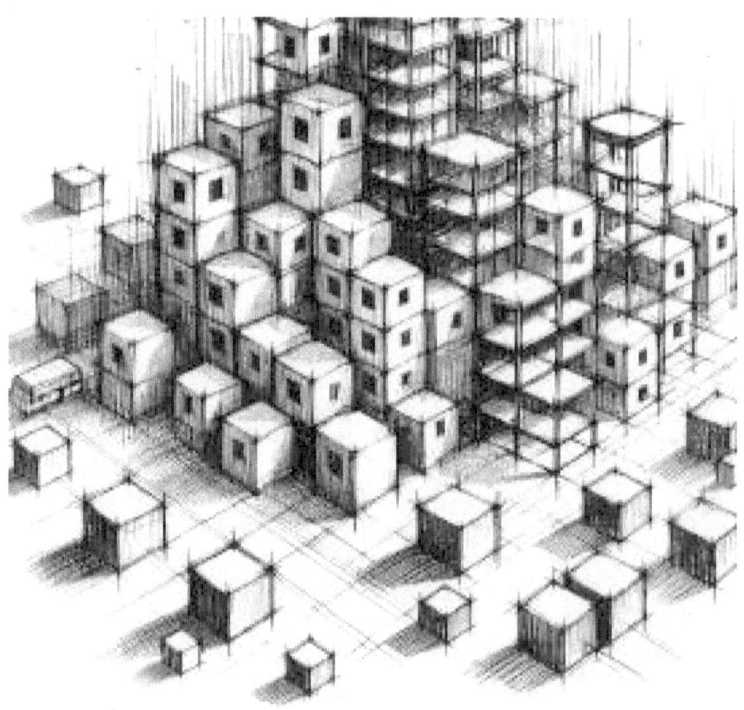

Avoid the Irrelevant

THERE IS A SIMPLE "DIET" YOU'D NEED TO FOLLOW TO BECOME & REMAIN SUPERCHARGED

▶ ▶ ▶ ▶ **AVOID THE IRRELEVANT** ◀ ◀ ◀ ◀

Everyone agrees that our time on this planet is limited. The exact amount? None of us know. Now imagine being led into a supermarket and told you have an unknown amount of time to grab whatever you want, but the catch is that you'll be kicked out without warning and can't take anything with you when the time is up. What would you do? Would you waste time exploring trivial items or focus entirely on grabbing that one dream of yours—the thing that energizes you and leaves a legacy after you're gone?

This analogy captures the essence of the principle: "Avoid the Irrelevant." Here's why this is crucial and how to implement it:

Why Avoiding the Irrelevant Matters

1. **Time is Finite:** Every moment spent on distractions is a moment stolen from your larger goal. You can't get it back.

2. **Attention is a Precious Resource:** Studies show that attention is a finite mental currency. When split across multiple tasks or distractions, its effectiveness diminishes. Focusing on irrelevant matters saps the energy needed for meaningful progress.

3. **Legacy Over Trivia:** What you leave behind is determined by what you invest in today. Scrolling social media or engaging in gossip rarely builds legacies.

How to Identify and Avoid the Irrelevant

1. Clarify Your Priorities

Before you can avoid distractions, you need to know what's important. Define your big-picture goals—the ones that excite you and align with your purpose.

Example: If your dream is to start a business, then binging random YouTube videos about unrelated topics becomes *noise*.

2. Be Ruthless with Distractions

Social media, gossip, or endless entertainment might feel good in the moment, but they pull you away from meaningful work.

Tip: Use tools like timers, app blockers, or digital detox periods to minimize exposure to irrelevant distractions.

3. Apply the Noise Filter

The word "distraction" literally means anything that pulls away from the action you intend to take. It's like trying to tune into RedFM while another channel's broadcast creates static interference. That interference is irrelevant noise.

Tip: Filter your environment and choices. If something doesn't add value to your primary goal, it's a distraction.

4. Choose People Wisely

Interacting with the wrong crowd can derail your focus. Surround yourself with individuals who align with your aspirations and values. Evaluate relationships: Are they helping or hindering your journey?

▶▶ How to choose your friends?

You Are the Average of the Five People You Spend the Most Time With

— Jim Rohn

This statement serves as a powerful reminder of the impact that those closest to us have on our growth, mindset, and overall quality of life. Choosing your circle wisely can determine whether you thrive or stagnate.

Les Brown famously advised focusing on **Only Quality People (OQP)** when cultivating relationships.

Why? Because the people you associate with most often shape your attitudes, habits, and ultimately, your outcomes. The company you keep can either elevate or drag you down.

How to Spot OQPs:
The quote by Eleanor Roosevelt provides a simple yet effective litmus test:

**Great minds discuss Ideas;
Average minds discuss Events;
Small minds discuss People.**

1. Small Minds (People Gossipers):
Observe the content of conversations. If the discussion revolves around people—who did what, why someone failed, or constant judgment—it reflects a focus on gossip and criticism. This mindset rarely fosters personal growth.

2. Average Minds (Event Followers):
Conversations centered on events—what happened at the latest party, yesterday's football match, or news headlines—are a step up but still lack the depth required for transformative growth.

3. Great Minds (Idea Generators):
If someone frequently discusses ideas—solutions, plans, visions, innovations, and ways to grow—they belong to the category of "great minds." These are the people who encourage, challenge, and inspire you to achieve your goals.

Look for Value Alignment

Choosing great minds isn't enough. The next step is ensuring value alignment. Shared values create a foundation for mutual understanding, trust, and support.

For example: If you value honesty but a potential friend doesn't, misunderstandings or conflicts may arise. Synergistic relationships are built on shared principles and the ability to reinforce each other's growth.

Questions to Evaluate OQP Potential

Here's a simple framework to determine whether someone qualifies as an OQP:

- What do they prioritize? Are they growth-oriented, or do they dwell in negativity?
- Do they challenge you constructively? Do they inspire you to think bigger and take bold action?
- Are they supportive yet honest? True OQPs encourage you but also provide constructive feedback.

- Are their values compatible with yours? Do they live by principles you respect or aspire to adopt?

The Advantages of Positive Association

Mindset: Surrounding yourself with uplifting individuals trains your brain to focus on possibilities, not limitations.

Behavior: You naturally pick up habits, attitudes, and standards from those around you.

Energy: Positive associations boost your motivation, while toxic relationships sap your energy.

Actionable Steps:

Audit Your Circle: List the five people you spend the most time with. Evaluate whether they uplift or hold you back.

Upgrade Gradually: Seek mentors, role models, and peers who embody the traits you want to cultivate. Start small, like attending events or online communities where OQPs gather.

Your network can act as your greatest asset or your biggest liability. Choose wisely, because your relationships can ultimately determine the trajectory of your life.

A Few Analogies to Reinforce the Idea

Water vs. Firehose: Trying to absorb everything—whether it's information, opinions, or tasks—is like drinking from a firehose. Instead, focus on the clear, direct stream that nourishes your goals.

The Gardener's Approach: Think of your life as a garden. Trim the weeds (irrelevant tasks) so your flowers (dreams) can bloom.

A Gentle Reminder for the Overachievers

Not all distractions are bad. Some are necessary for rest and recovery. The goal isn't to eliminate leisure or fun entirely but to ensure these don't take over. Strike a balance by allocating time intentionally for relaxation, ensuring it doesn't compete with your primary purpose.

By avoiding the irrelevant, you'll free up the time and mental energy needed to pursue what truly matters. So, whether it's tackling that next milestone or just being fully present in the moment, make every choice count. After all, life's supermarket doesn't give refunds on wasted time.

"Whatever you're unwilling to give up will inevitably be the thing that slows you down from achieving your dreams. If that list is too long, it becomes highly unlikely that you'll accomplish anything truly significant. By eliminating the vices that hold you back, you create the space needed to grow and become more"

— Dan Martell

Your Evolution is Your Responsibility

We don't rise to the standards we have when others are watching. We fall to the standards we have when no one is watching. The only work that really matters is the work that no one sees. It shows you who you really are, rather than who you say you are.

Continuously and relentlessly challenge yourself to reinvent, upgrade, and transform who you are. True growth begins from within, sparked by brutal yet honest introspection that shines a light on why you haven't yet reached the heights you aspire to. This self-awareness is not a sign of weakness but a stepping stone to greatness.

The most powerful tool for introspection is to ask yourself deep, meaningful questions and scribe your answers. As you pour your thoughts onto the page, you'll uncover not only what's holding you back but also the immense potential waiting to be unlocked within you. Remember, every small step of self-improvement brings you closer to becoming the best version of yourself.

💬 10 Questions to continuously ask yourself

Answer these questions and revisit and revise them in your notebook during your "ME Time."

1. If I was less afraid of people's opinions, what would I say?
2. What actually makes me happy?
3. Does Success make me happy?
4. What is my definition of Success?
5. What is my definition of Success if money was taken out of the equation?
6. What is my definition of Success if money and followers was taken out of the equation?
7. What are the things I would like to do forever, if money were not an object?
8. What are the things I am hiding from myself?
9. What are the emotions that I am unprepared to feel?
10. What are the things that I feel the most shame and guilt around?

💬 30,000 Feet Questions (Brooks, 2023)

Given below are some more questions you could imagine me asking you.

Answering and revisiting them would help you gain clarity on what your life should truly be about:

11. If the last five years were a chapter in your life, what would the chapter be about?
12. If we met a year from now, what would we be celebrating?
13. What would you do if you weren't afraid?
14. What is the "NO" or refusal you keep postponing?
15. What commitments have you made that you no longer believe in?
16. What is the gift you currently hold in exile?
17. What talent do you have that you're not using?

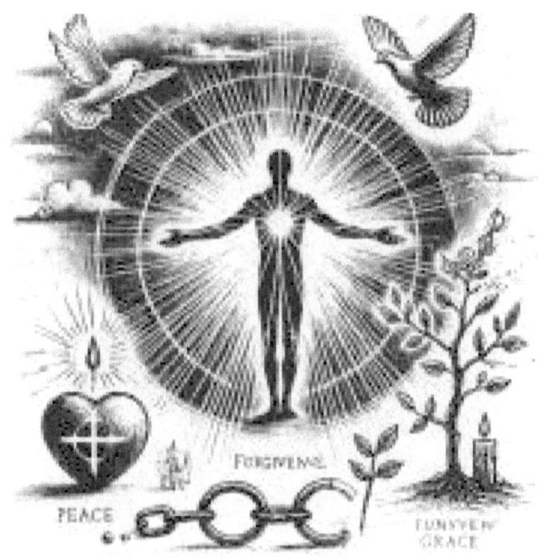

Lord, make me an instrument of your peace.

Where there is hatred, let me sow **Love**;
where there is injury, **Pardon**;
where there is doubt, **Faith**;
where there is despair, **Hope**;
where there is darkness, **Light**;
and where there is sadness, **Joy**.

O Divine Master, grant that I may not so much seek
to be consoled as to console;
to be understood as to understand;
to be loved as to love.
For it is in giving that we receive;
it is in pardoning that we are pardoned;
and it is in dying that we are born to eternal life.

St. Francis of Assisi

PART 3

GRATITUDE BLOCKERS

Superman has his Kryptonite, and gratitude, being the greatest superpower, also has its vices. To fully harness the power of gratitude, you must address certain overlooked factors. Often dismissed as trivial, these obstacles can prevent us from realizing our full potential. This chapter explores those barriers and offers strategies to overcome them.

Gratitude Blockers

What prevents Gratitude from flowing into our life?

To truly understand the factors that block gratitude from flourishing in our lives, it helps to examine them through the lens of time—specifically, the past, present, and future.

Let's begin by exploring how the past can prevent us from experiencing gratitude.

Blockers in The Past

There's a concept in Shamanism called *soul fragmentation*, which refers to the effects of trauma or deeply unpleasant events on a person. The belief is that when someone experiences a traumatic event, a part of their soul becomes fragmented and remains stuck in that moment. This part of the soul is unable to move forward, leaving the person incomplete, as if a piece of them remains anchored in that painful moment. In this state of fragmentation, the soul—our tool for achieving fulfillment and wholeness—loses its strength and capacity to support our full potential. Unless these lost fragments are reclaimed and reintegrated, the person is likely to continue living in a diminished state, unable to fully engage in life or reach their highest potential.

Resolving Past Gratitude Blockers

Let's consider an analogy: Imagine a ship setting sail across the ocean. When the ship needs to dock, it drops anchor, unloads cargo, takes on new supplies, lifts the anchor, and continues on its journey. But what happens if the ship's captain becomes emotionally attached to the port and refuses to raise the anchor? No matter how much they try to sail forward, the ship will remain stuck, anchored in place. Similarly, when we experience difficult or traumatic events, we often drop an emotional anchor at that moment. While it's important to pause and process what's happening, we sometimes refuse to lift that anchor, choosing instead to remain emotionally tied to the pain. In doing so, we prevent ourselves from moving forward, and our progress in life stalls.

The key to releasing these emotional anchors and reclaiming the fragmented pieces of our soul is through a process known as *healing*. Healing, like its physical counterpart, must take place on mental, emotional, and spiritual levels. While there are many techniques to achieve this—meditation, practices like Ho'oponopono, and more— the cornerstone of all healing is *forgiveness*.

Forgiveness isn't just about letting others off the hook; it's about freeing yourself from the chains of the past. Forgive yourself for the mistakes or choices you made. Forgive the people and situations that caused you pain. Understand that life's challenges are not punishments—they are lessons designed to help you grow and unleash your full potential, for both your own benefit and the benefit of the world.

An inspiring example of this transformative process is the story of Dr. Sunitha Krishnan, an Indian woman who overcame horrific trauma to become a powerful force for good. Dr. Krishnan is the founder of Prajwala, an NGO dedicated to rescuing and rehabilitating girls trapped in the world of sex trafficking. But before she became a champion for women's empowerment, Sunitha was an ordinary 15-year-old girl who experienced a brutal, life-altering event.

While working with an NGO to promote girls' education in rural areas, she encountered fierce opposition from local men who clung to outdated patriarchal traditions. These men, threatened by her efforts to empower women, viciously assaulted her. In that moment, Sunitha faced a critical decision: would she allow this horrific act to define and break her, or would she rise above it? She chose the latter.

Instead of letting the trauma shackle her to the past, Sunitha used it as fuel to drive her mission of fighting for justice. Today, she is a beacon of hope for women across the world. Her story is a powerful reminder that while we may not have control over what happens to us, we always have control over how we respond. Sunitha's ability to heal, forgive, and move forward enabled her to transform her life— and the lives of thousands of others.

The lesson here is simple: if you want to live a life filled with gratitude, you must let go of the anchors from your past. Reclaim the fragmented parts of your soul by embracing forgiveness, healing, and understanding that even the hardest moments serve a higher purpose in shaping your greatness. By doing so, you free yourself to experience the fullness of gratitude in the present.

Have you ever noticed how your PC becomes painfully sluggish when you have 100 Google Chrome tabs open? Each of those tabs consumes valuable computing power that could be better used for something more productive. Similarly, unresolved or unhealed issues act like open files in your mental "computer," draining your mental and emotional energy just to keep them running in the background.

To avoid creating new *anchors* as you go through life, make it a habit to resolve issues as soon as they arise. You know those times when a lingering thought urges you to speak up after being unfairly reprimanded, or when someone crosses a boundary and hurts you, even if they think it's just a harmless joke; these are files that stay open and consume your personal power.

Be open and assertive—express yourself clearly and honestly. Clear and close the *file* so that you don't carry it around unnecessarily. Address the issue, resolve it, and free your mental space for what truly matters.

▶▶ My Mental Reset Button

A personal favorite for clearing out the mental clutter has been Ho'oponopono, a Hawaiian practice for forgiveness and healing that feels like a spiritual cleaning crew for your inner world. For me, it's been nothing short of magical—like a mental Marie Kondo process, but instead of folding socks, you're folding up old grudges and tossing them out. I've often been stunned by the mountain of emotional "junk" I've unearthed, thinking, *Wow, how did THAT get in here?*

At its heart, Ho'oponopono is wonderfully simple—no yoga mat or crystals required. Just four phrases:

1. **I'm Sorry.** (For whatever I did, knowingly or unknowingly—yes, even that time I ate the last slice of pizza.)
2. **Please Forgive Me.**
3. **Thank You.** (For putting up with me while I figure things out.)
4. **I Love You.** (To myself, the universe, or my Wi-Fi connection for holding it together during stressful Zoom calls.)

<u>**How to Practice:**</u>

Set an Intention: Focus on something that's bugging you—a relationship, a past mistake, or even the annoyance of stepping on a LEGO barefoot.

Repeat the Phrases: Say them in your head, aloud, or even while muttering into your coffee. Direct the energy inward, toward a person, or a situation, and feel the emotions behind the words.

Let Go: No, really—stop overthinking. Just keep repeating the phrases and trust the magic to do its thing. Think of it as rebooting your emotional system—Ctrl+Alt+Delete for the soul.

What's incredible is you don't need anyone else to join in. It's not like karaoke night—this is your solo healing jam. Ho'oponopono works because it's all about taking responsibility for what's in your emotional space, clearing out the negativity, and replacing it with peace and clarity.

It's quick, transformative, and oddly satisfying. Try it—you might just find yourself thanking and loving things you never thought you could (yes, even that LEGO).

If someone has wronged me, hurt me, or caused me any loss, my personal practice is to *always plot and exact my revenge.* Now, before you gasp and clutch your pearls, let me explain. My approach to revenge is a little… *Unconventional.*

Here's how it works: I carefully observe my "target" and take note of the areas in their life where they seem to be struggling. Is their career stuck? Relationships fraying? Confidence low? I pinpoint those struggles, and then I strike—*HARD.*

But NOT in the way you're thinking.

In my prayers and conversations with The Almighty, I unleash my "revenge" by asking, pleading, and downright insisting that every single one of their problems gets resolved in the most magnificent way possible. I pray that the Almighty showers them with unimaginable blessings, that their dreams come true, and that they're given all the joy, success, and clarity they could ever want. Oh, and as a bonus, I ask Him to grant us both realization and wisdom, so we can become better humans—and possibly even friends!

Why do I do this? First, because it's hilariously freeing. Instead of stewing over their wrongdoing, I mentally high-five myself for *out-nicing* them. Second, it clears up all that precious mental space I'd otherwise waste on bitterness. Instead of obsessing over someone who isn't paying rent to live in my head, I get to focus on my growth, happiness, and maybe my next book.

And on a lighter note, when I see my "victim" thriving and glowing up, I smile smugly to myself and tell him in my mind, "You're welcome. That's all me, buddy. Enjoy!"

Blockers in The Present

What factors in our present life block gratitude from flowing freely?

Let's explore this by imagining a light bulb connected to three fuses. If all three fuses are strong and intact, the light bulb shines brightly. If one fuse is weak, the light will flicker. And if any fuse is completely blown, the bulb won't light up at all.

Similarly, there are three critical people in your life who act like fuses in your connection to the Source of energy that drives your growth and fulfillment. These three people are your Mother (Matha), Father (Pitha), and Teacher (Guru). If there are unresolved issues with any of these individuals, it can create significant blocks in your life.

Even when opportunities present themselves, you might find yourself falling short, facing inexplicable setbacks, or struggling to achieve your goals. Despite your talents and hard work, you may hear people say, "You should be so much further along," and wonder what's holding you back.

How These Blocks Manifest

1. **Unresolved Issues with Your Mother**

   If you have unresolved emotional issues with your mother, this will often manifest in your relationships with others. You may find it hard to connect with people, trust them, or build meaningful, lasting relationships. You might struggle with feeling isolated or unable to create the close bonds that bring richness to life.

2. **Unresolved Issues with Your Father**

   Issues with your father can manifest as problems in your career, financial life, and achievements. When you set out to accomplish something, you may find yourself constantly coming up short or encountering roadblocks that seem insurmountable. You may be working hard, but the results never seem to match your efforts.

3. **Unresolved Issues with Your Teacher**

   Problems with your teacher or mentor will block your ability to fully utilize the knowledge and skills you've gained. You might excel academically or professionally, but when the moment comes to apply what you know, you find yourself either forgetting it or unable to use it effectively. It's like owning a treasure chest but not having the key to open it.

<u>Resolving Present Gratitude Blockers</u>

So how do you resolve these seemingly unresolvable issues? The key lies in genuinely reconnecting with these three categories of people—Mother, Father, and Teacher—and healing those relationships from the heart.

1. **Have an Open-Hearted Conversation**

    If your parents or teachers are still alive, initiate a conversation. Speak with them openly, clearing the air of any resentment or misunderstandings you may be holding onto. Seek their blessings, not as a transaction, but as a step toward emotional healing and resolution. Whether or not they reciprocate, you will have done your part by restoring integrity to the relationship from your side. Become that 5-year-old kid again, eagerly looking up to your parents with wonder and admiration. (Use the concept of *5 Love Languages* to understand their style of love).

    > Find out what they love to talk about, ask them about it, and then listen with the wide-eyed excitement of a 5-year-old hearing it for the first time—complete with the "Wow!" face!

2. **If They Are No Longer Alive**

If your parents or teachers have passed on, you can still heal these relationships. Treat their friends and relatives with respect and kindness, honoring the legacy of your parents or mentors. Once a week, sit quietly with your eyes closed and visualize your mother, father, or teacher in front of you. In this mental space, ask for forgiveness and imagine them placing their hand on your head in a gesture of blessing. Feel the warmth and energy of their blessing flowing through you, restoring the connection.

I believe that when we remember someone close to us who has passed on, it's not just a sign—it's them gently tapping us on the shoulder (or smacking us on the back of the head, depending on their personality) to remind us to keep their legacy alive.

And how do we do that?

Every person comes to this world with their own quirky, unique "user manual" of life lessons to share—whether through their actions, words, or the ridiculous yet heartwarming things they used to do, like insisting pizza crust was the healthiest part.

Our job, as the ones still kicking around here, is to carry forward their lessons. Share their stories, live their values, and pass on the wisdom they left behind. It's like becoming the ambassador for their greatest hits album, except instead of gold records, you're spreading goodness. When someone starts adopting those lessons, you can be rest assured that your dear one is alive in spirit as an **Idea**—living on through the goodness they've sparked in others.

And here's the bonus: by spreading their values, you become part of a kindness chain reaction. It's like a pyramid scheme, but instead of getting people to sell essential oils, you're multiplying goodness. Imagine a world where this positivity keeps growing, sparking joy in people who never even knew your loved one. What a magical, hilarious, and heartwarming way to keep their spirit alive!

Become a Clear path for the Energy to Flow

Just as we need to resolve these blocks to receive energy, we also have a responsibility to pass that energy forward to the next generation. Whether you have children of your own or play a guiding  role in someone's life, bless those who come after you. Visualize them becoming the best version of themselves. Your role in their lives is to empower them with love, encouragement, and positivity, allowing the energy to flow through you and continue the cycle of growth and gratitude. By healing these key relationships and allowing energy to flow freely through your life, you clear the way for gratitude to take root and grow. This practice not only reconnects you to the people who shaped you but also ensures that you are a source of love and support for those who come after you.

One powerful tool I have found particularly useful for understanding and improving relationships is the concept of Love Languages introduced by Dr. Gary Chapman, a marriage counselor, pastoral theologian, and author, who first introduced this groundbreaking relationship framework in his 1992 book "The Five Love Languages"

Dr. Chapman recognized that people express and receive love in different ways, which he likened to speaking distinct "emotional languages." Just as successful verbal communication depends on understanding each other's spoken language, emotional communication depends on understanding each other's love language.

Key Principles

1. **Different Ways of Expressing Love:** Each person has a primary love language—a specific way they most feel loved and appreciated. This "language" develops naturally through life experiences and emotional makeup rather than being consciously learned.

2. **Primary and Secondary Love Languages:** While people tend to have one dominant love language, they also have a secondary one that shapes how they express or interpret love. For instance, someone may feel most loved through acts of service but also enjoy quality time as a close second.

3. **Miscommunication Creates Gaps:** Misunderstandings often arise when people "speak" different love languages. For example, one person might express love by giving gifts, but their partner might primarily value quality time. As a result, the recipient might feel unloved even though love is present—just expressed differently.

4. **Not Just for Romance:** The love languages framework isn't limited to romantic relationships. It applies to family dynamics, friendships, workplace connections, and even self-love. By understanding these languages, relationships across all spheres can grow stronger.

When applied thoughtfully, love languages can heal rifts by ensuring that love and appreciation are communicated effectively. By identifying and "speaking" love languages effectively, relationships can transform from strained to thriving, creating bonds that feel both supportive and fulfilling.

1. **Improved Emotional Connection:** Understanding how someone feels loved allows you to express your affection in ways that truly resonate with them. For instance, if your mom's love language is acts of service, helping her clean the house may mean more than buying her an expensive gift.

2. **Reduced Misunderstandings:** Being aware of love languages minimizes feelings of neglect or frustration. For example, if your sibling values quality time, they won't feel dismissed when you prioritize spending undistracted moments with them.

3. **Enhanced Self-Awareness:** Recognizing your own love language helps you communicate your needs clearly. If you feel undervalued in relationships, identifying your love language can help you pinpoint and express what's missing.

4. **Better Conflict Resolution:** Love languages help address disagreements constructively. If your dad complains about you not calling often (quality time), you can resolve this by scheduling regular check-ins.

The five love languages identified by Chapman are:

1. **Words of Affirmation:** People who value verbal expressions of love, compliments, encouragement, and appreciation. They feel most loved when receiving kind, supportive, and specific verbal acknowledgments.

2. **Acts of Service:** Individuals who feel most loved when someone does helpful things for them. Practical assistance, completing tasks, and providing support are their primary love expressions.

3. **Receiving Gifts:** These individuals interpret gifts as tangible symbols of love. The emotional thought and effort behind the gift matter more than its monetary value.

4. **Quality Time:** People who feel most connected when receiving undivided attention. Meaningful conversations, shared experiences, and focused interaction are their primary love indicators.

5. **Physical Touch:** Individuals who feel most loved through physical affection like hugs, kisses, holding hands, and physical proximity.

Understanding your parents' love languages can be a transformative journey towards healing and strengthening your relationship. The 5 Love Languages concept help you do exactly that.

Here is one way of decoding and connecting with your parents through their unique love language expression:

Words of Affirmation Parents: These parents typically express and receive love through verbal communication. They deeply value hearing specific, genuine praise and emotional validation.

To connect, start by actively listening to their stories, offering sincere compliments about their life achievements, and verbally expressing your appreciation for their efforts.

Pay attention to how they communicate – do they frequently offer advice, share stories, or seek verbal validation?

If they light up when you acknowledge their wisdom or express gratitude for their life lessons, this might be their primary love language.

Acts of Service Parents: For these parents, love is demonstrated through practical help and support. They feel most appreciated when you anticipate their needs and offer tangible assistance. This might look like helping with household chores, running errands, assisting with technology, or providing practical support during challenging times.

Notice if they constantly do things for you or others – this is likely how they express love.

To connect, ask about tasks they're struggling with or proactively offer help without being asked.

Receiving Gifts Parents: These parents view gifts as tangible expressions of love and memory. The emotional value trumps the monetary cost. They often keep sentimental items and appreciate thoughtful, meaningful presents that show you've been paying attention to their interests. The key is not about expensive gifts, but gifts that demonstrate deep understanding.

Notice if they frequently give you gifts or cherish family heirlooms – this might indicate their love language.

Quality Time Parents: For these parents, undivided attention is the ultimate expression of love. They value deep conversations, shared experiences, and genuine presence. This means putting away phones, creating dedicated time for interaction, and truly listening.

If they frequently try to engage you in conversations, plan family activities, or seem hurt when you're distracted, quality time is likely their primary love language.

Physical Touch Parents: These parents express and receive love through physical affection like hugs, kisses, gentle touches, or simply being physically close.

If they frequently try to touch you, stand close, or feel comfortable with physical proximity, this might be their love language. For those with more reserved parents, even small gestures of physical connection can be powerful.

Practical Steps to Reconnect:
1. Observe their natural communication and interaction patterns
2. Reflect on past interactions that made them visibly happy
3. Experiment with expressing love in different ways
4. Have an open, honest conversation about feelings
5. Practice patience and consistency

Healing Approach:
1. Approach with empathy and without judgment
2. Understand that your parents are complex individuals with their own emotional histories
3. Recognize that love languages can be learned and evolved
4. Be willing to be vulnerable and share your own emotional journey

Potential Challenges:
1. Some parents might have difficulty expressing or receiving love due to generational or cultural barriers
2. Past traumas or unresolved conflicts might complicate love language interpretation
3. Different love language styles can create misunderstandings

Professional Guidance:
Consider family therapy or counseling if:
1. Communication remains consistently challenging
2. Deep-seated emotional wounds exist
3. You need mediated support in understanding each other

The 5 Love Languages tool is invaluable for strengthening bonds with ANYONE, be it parents, children, spouses, friends, or even colleagues. By identifying and "speaking" the love languages of those closest to us, we can build relationships based on mutual understanding, trust, and genuine connection.

Blockers in The Future

The future, despite its endless possibilities and opportunities, is often viewed with anxiety, apprehension, and fear of the unknown. Many of us spend more time worrying about what *might* happen rather than embracing the potential it holds.

There's a joke that illustrates this: *When is the population of a country at its lowest?* Most people would try to guess a specific date or time. But the answer is, "At present." The reasoning is that most people are either living regretfully in the past or anxiously fearing the future. The few who remain are glued to their devices, living in cyberspace. So effectively, the "present" is sparsely populated! If a hostile force were to invade, the "past-dwellers" and "future-worriers" wouldn't even notice until it was too late.

The future blocks gratitude in our lives through the anxiousness we harbor about outcomes that haven't even happened yet—perhaps over things we haven't even begun. We lose the only time we truly have—**the present**—to fears about something that may or may not occur. Ironically, the only way to create a better future is by acting in the present. The more time we spend oscillating between regret over the past and worry about the future, the more we trap ourselves in inaction, thus setting ourselves up for a future filled with exactly the things we fear.

Resolving Future Gratitude Blockers

One powerful way to dissolve these future blocks is to express gratitude in advance for the outcome you desire. Instead of anxiously focusing on what could go wrong, focus on the present and thank the people, circumstances, and forces in advance, as though they've already helped you achieve your ideal outcome. For example, if you're about to embark on a journey, instead of worrying about all the things that could go wrong, thank the universe, the people involved, and all the circumstances for guiding you safely to your destination. This shift in mindset not only calms your anxiety but also seems to help manifest the desired outcome in a nearly magical way.

Another important practice when thinking about the future is to embrace trust in the process. As we discussed earlier, there is an All-Knowing, All-Powerful Higher Power guiding us toward becoming the best version of ourselves. This journey not only elevates us but also contributes to the greater good of the world. When you set a goal or make a plan for the future, try adding the clause: *"this or something better."* This small addition signals to the Higher Power that while you have a clear intention, you also trust that what is best for you—something you may not even be aware of—will come to pass.

In doing so, you shift from fear and control toward gratitude and trust. You've made your wishes known, but you are also open to receiving something beyond your current imagination—something that may better serve your highest good.

When you let go of anxiousness and approach the future with gratitude, you begin to see possibilities instead of limitations. By focusing on the present and acting with faith, you create a life where gratitude flows effortlessly, and the future, rather than being a source of fear, becomes a field of opportunity where "this or something better" awaits you

YOU CAN'T GO BACK AND CHANGE THE BEGINNING,

BUT YOU CAN START WHERE YOU ARE AND CHANGE THE ENDING

C. S LEWIS

PART 4

GRATITUDE FOREVER

Gratitude isn't just a one-time practice—it's a way of living, a vital force to be woven into the fabric of your everyday existence. That's why this chapter dives into practical exercises, meaningful rituals, and transformative habits to help you fully embrace gratitude. Get ready to turn it into a powerful, daily energy source that keeps you unstoppable!

The Three Processes of Transformation

An individual is not a fragmented entity but a harmonious blend of three interconnected "MBA" elements: Mind, Body, and Athma (Soul). To become truly strong, resilient, and empowered, we must nurture and energize all three levels. When these elements are in balance, we unlock our full potential and experience a sense of wholeness. This is not just about well-being; it's about thriving in every aspect of life. To strengthen these elements, we need to focus on three universal processes:

1. **Creation**:
   This is the beginning of empowering practices—mindsets, habits, and routines that uplift and energize your Mind, Body, and Athma. Creation is about adding value to your life by intentionally cultivating positive and transformative practices.

2. **Sustenance**:
   It's not enough to create; what you create must be nurtured and maintained. Sustenance is the commitment to consistency, the discipline to stick with your empowering practices even when life challenges you.

3. **Destruction**:
   To grow, we must let go of what no longer serves us. Destruction is the act of releasing disempowering habits, toxic mindsets, and limiting beliefs. It clears the path for creation and sustenance to flourish.

IT DOES NOT MATTER HOW SLOWLY YOU GO
SO LONG AS YOU DO NOT STOP

CONFUCIOUS

Energizing The Three Elements

Each of the processes — Creation, Sustenance, and Destruction — should be applied to the Mind, Body, and Athma, to ensure sustainable holistic growth:

ELEMENT	CREATION	SUSTENANCE	DESTRUCTION
MIND	Introduce mindfulness, gratitude, and positive affirmations into your daily life.	Maintain focus through meditation, journaling, and mental clarity practices.	Eliminate self-doubt, overthinking, and toxic thought patterns.
BODY	Build physical strength and vitality through regular exercise, nutrition, and sleep.	Sustain energy by practicing consistency in movement and balanced routines.	Break free from unhealthy habits like overindulgence or neglecting self-care.
ATHMA	Explore spiritual practices such as prayer, meditation, and acts of kindness.	Nurture your soul by staying aligned with your values and engaging in moments of stillness.	Let go of guilt, regret, and anything that blocks spiritual growth.

This chapter is your invitation to start. To *plan, do, check,* and *act* on your life. To take deliberate steps to weave gratitude into your everyday moments, gradually but firmly, until it becomes an inseparable part of who you are.

Here are a few concepts you would need to know in the journey forward.

Gratitude Routines : Simple practices to incorporate into your daily life. Over time, these will take on a life of their own, becoming habits that naturally keep your life supercharged.

Gratitude Rituals : Special practices for special occasions. These rituals will help you amplify your gratitude, making important moments in your life even more meaningful and transformative.

Gratitude Meditation : A mindfulness practice that helps you center your heart and mind, fostering a deeper connection to gratitude and the present moment.

Gratitude Retreat: A transformative break for self-discovery to step away from daily pressures and reconnect with inner peace. Through mindful practices and reflection, you cultivate deep appreciation, shedding stress and emerging with renewed energy and a profoundly grateful perspective.

Gratitude Routines

We are what we consistently do. Our habits, whether empowering or disempowering, have shaped the path that has brought us to this moment. If we desire a life far more beautiful, purposeful, and extraordinary than the one we are currently living, we must cultivate new habits that align with the future we envision.

Habits may seem like small, trivial parts of our daily routines—so small that we often overlook their profound cumulative impact. Yet, they are the foundation of everything we achieve, or fail to achieve, in life. The key to living a supercharged life lies in mastering our habits: creating new, empowering habits, sustaining and refining existing "good" habits, and breaking free from those that hold us back.

While a comprehensive analysis of habits—how they are formed and how to transform them—is beyond the scope of this book (perhaps the subject of a sequel!), it is enough to say this: to supercharge your life, you must focus on your habits. Small, intentional changes, made consistently, have the power to transform your life in ways you may never have thought possible. The time to start is NOW!

I've drawn insights from James Clear's Atomic Habits and BJ Fogg's Tiny Habits to help you build sustainable gratitude habits that lead to purpose, joy, and fulfillment. These proven strategies are most effective when approached with joy and love, not as chores. The more you genuinely enjoy the practice, the more transformative it becomes. Let gratitude be an uplifting celebration of life's beauty—where every small action brings you closer to the extraordinary life you deserve. Root these principles in your daily life and watch gratitude transform your mindset and your world.

Anchor Gratitude in the Present Moment:

Gratitude is most powerful when anchored to the "now," focusing on life's gifts in the present moment. By centering your attention on what is happening here and now, you amplify the power of gratitude.

Actionable Tip: Before starting, repeat: "Right now, I am grateful for..." to center your focus on the current moment.

Combine Gratitude with Deep Breathing

Slow, intentional breathing helps create a calm mental state, making it easier to connect with gratitude. Synchronize your thoughts of gratitude with each breath to deepen its effect.

Actionable Tip: Practice the 4-7-8 breathing technique while visualizing something or someone you are thankful for.

Make Gratitude a Daily Habit

Consistency is key to harnessing the full transformative power of gratitude. Pairing gratitude meditation with an existing daily habit makes it easier to maintain regular practice.

Actionable Tip: Use reminders, like a sticky note or alarm, to dedicate a consistent time for gratitude meditation each day.

Visualize Gratitude for Emotional Impact

Visualization enhances the emotional depth of gratitude by making it more vivid and heartfelt. Imagine specific moments, people, or experiences you are grateful for to strengthen the connection.

Actionable Tip: Visualize each point of gratitude as a growing light within you, expanding with each breath and creating a sense of warmth.

Release Judgment and Redirect Focus

Distractions are a natural part of meditation. Instead of resisting them, acknowledge their presence without judgment and gently bring your focus back to gratitude.

Actionable Tip: When distracted, say: "I see you, but I choose gratitude," and return to your chosen point of focus.

Some Gratitude Routines

♥ Gratitude Journal

This is the most common gratitude practice and requires just a notebook, a pen, and about 10 minutes of your time right before bed. I recommend investing in a special notebook or diary dedicated solely to this purpose and keeping it near your bedside table for convenience. This practice should ideally be the last thing you do before falling asleep.

Each night, write down 10 things you're thankful for. These don't need to be grand or life-changing—small, everyday things work just as well. For instance, it could be as simple as "I'm thankful for strawberry ice cream."

Tips for an Effective Gratitude Journal

Avoid Repetition: Make it a point not to repeat the same items. For example, if you've already written about being thankful for strawberry ice cream once, move on to something new. This forces your mind to scan for fresh things to be grateful for, sharpening your awareness of life's blessings. While this may feel challenging at first, it becomes second nature over time.

Amplify the Feeling: After listing your items, revisit each one and deepen the associated feeling or memory. Let's say you're grateful for strawberry ice cream—recall its taste, texture, and the joy it brought you. Fully immerse yourself in that sensation, amplifying it until it feels overwhelming. At the peak of that happiness, express heartfelt gratitude by saying "Thank you" for the experience.

The Science Behind Gratitude Journalling

Subconscious Programming: By making this the last thing you do before sleep, your positive thoughts seep into your subconscious mind, setting the tone for how your brain processes emotions and memories overnight.

The Reticular Activating System (RAS): This part of your brain acts as a filter, spotlighting what it deems important. Consider the "red car effect"—how many red cars did you notice on your drive home? Likely, not many. But if someone promised to pay you $10 for each red car you see, suddenly, the streets would seem flooded with them. The cars were always there; your RAS simply wasn't prioritizing them. Similarly, when you train your mind to scan for things to be grateful for, you'll begin to notice an abundance of blessings that were previously overlooked.

  ## Gratitude Stone

Find a smooth, shiny pocket-sized stone or marble and carry it with you at all times. This stone serves as a powerful reminder. Every time you see or touch it, take a moment to think of something you're grateful for and express your heartfelt gratitude. If your gratitude is directed toward a person, go the extra mile by communicating it to them, explaining why you're thankful.

I also give the stone an additional purpose: it becomes my "positivity power bank." When I'm feeling happy or energized—when I'm vibrating at my highest frequency—I hold the stone in my hand and imagine that positive energy getting stored into it. Later, when I touch the stone again, whether intentionally or accidentally, I visualize a burst of that stored energy coursing through me, instantly uplifting my mood.

In this way, the stone becomes my real-life philosopher's stone, transforming any moment into one of empowerment and positivity.

💜 21-Day Gratitude Detox

For 21 days, refrain from all things that disempower you. This practice should be closely aligned with the principles outlined in "Avoid the Irrelevant." Below is a partial list of things to avoid, but it is not exhaustive. You can decide whether something needs to be removed based on how it affects your energy and focus.

For beginners, refrain from the four vices: Blaming, Complaining, Criticizing, and Gossiping for 21 days. If you slip into any of these vices, don't despair. Simply restart your countdown and begin again. Once you've successfully completed 21 days in the "beginner" mode, choose one or two more items from the list and add them to your "no-do" list, then start another 21-day detox cycle.

1. **Negativity:** Avoid negative media, pessimistic conversations, or people who drain your energy.
2. **Social Media Overload:** Refrain from excessive social media use, particularly before bed and in the morning.
3. **Gossiping:** Steer clear of gossip, as it feeds negative thinking and disrupts positive focus.

4. **Complaints:** Avoid complaining, as it shifts focus away from gratitude and empowerment.

5. **Criticism:** Refrain from unnecessary criticism of others, and focus on constructive feedback.

6. **Overthinking:** Limit overanalyzing situations that drain your energy.

7. **News Consumption:** Avoid consuming negative or overwhelming news first thing in the morning or before bedtime.

8. **Procrastination:** Stop putting off important tasks, as it leads to stress and wasted time.

9. **Toxic Environments:** Stay away from environments or individuals that bring negativity into your life.

10. **Doomscrolling:** Avoid mindlessly scrolling through social media or news feeds, especially when it feeds anxiety or fear.

11. **Multitasking:** Focus on one task at a time, allowing yourself to fully engage and appreciate the moment.

12. **Avoiding Self-Care:** Don't neglect your mental or physical well-being. Prioritize activities that nurture your body and mind.

13. **People-Pleasing:** Say no to people or commitments that drain your energy and distract you from your own goals.

14. **Wasteful Consumption:** Be mindful of how you spend your time, money, and attention. Avoid overindulgence in activities or purchases that don't add value to your life.

15. **Negative Self-Talk:** Replace critical inner dialogue with affirmations and positive reinforcement.

16. **Staying in Comfort Zones:** Challenge yourself to grow by stepping out of your comfort zone.

17. **Excessive Comparisons:** Avoid comparing yourself to others on social media or in real life, focusing instead on your own unique path.

18. **Unnecessary Drama:** Refrain from getting involved in unnecessary conflicts or situations that cause emotional turmoil.

19. **Bad Habits:** Identify and refrain from any habits that hinder your personal growth or diminish your sense of empowerment.

20. **Sleep Disruptions:** Avoid late-night activities or habits that interfere with restful sleep.

21. **Unfocused Routines:** Avoid sticking to routines that don't serve your well-being or personal development.

This list is not exhaustive. It is just a starting point, but it's important to recognize your own areas of disempowerment and decide what to eliminate to create more room for positivity, growth, and empowerment.

This practice is a recommended add-on to the "Avoid the Irrelevant"explained before.

5 More Gratitude Routines

Gratitude is not a one-size-fits-all practice—it can be flexible, fun, and deeply personal. Start small, stay consistent, and enjoy the positive ripple effects that gratitude can create in your life. These practices are simple enough for anyone to start today and meaningful enough to transform your mindset in the long term.

Practice #1: The 3-2-1 Evening Reflection

Why it's powerful: This practice links gratitude to your everyday life, enhances self-awareness, and ends your day on a positive note.

Steps:

Before bed, write down:

- 3 small things that happened today
- 2 people who made your day better
- 1 thing you're proud of about yourself

Key points for effectiveness:

- Be specific (e.g., instead of "family," write "Mom's encouraging text this morning")
- Aim for different answers each day
- Appreciate even tiny things (a warm cup of coffee, a smile from a stranger)
- Write by hand if possible
- Keep supplies by your bedside to make it easy

Practice #2: The Thank You Walk

Why it's powerful: It blends physical activity, mindfulness, and gratitude, making it an effortless part of your daily routine.

Steps:

During a regular walk (to work, during lunch, etc.), focus on a different category of gratitude each day:

- **Monday:** Nature
- **Tuesday:** Your body
- **Wednesday:** Opportunities
- **Thursday:** People
- **Friday:** Personal growth

Key points for effectiveness:

- Leave your phone behind—no distractions

- Identify at least 5 things to be grateful for as you walk

- Think or say them in complete sentences

- Breathe deeply, tune into your body, and notice how gratitude changes your mood

Practice #3: The Gratitude Ripple

Why it's powerful: This practice creates a positive feedback loop, strengthens relationships, and naturally spreads gratitude.

Steps:

- Each morning, choose one person to thank
- Send them a short message (text, email, or note)
- Be specific about what they did and how it positively affected you
- Ask about their well-being to foster connection

Key points for effectiveness:

- Be genuine—don't force it
- Focus on recent events whenever possible
- Recognize both big and small acts of kindness
- Follow up if they respond, but don't expect anything in return

Practice #4: The Contrast Method

Why it's powerful: It helps overcome negativity bias, builds resilience, and deepens appreciation for what you have.

Steps:

When you're facing a challenge, pause and:

- List 3 ways the situation could be worse
- Identify 2 hidden benefits in the current situation
- Find 1 lesson or opportunity for growth
- Express gratitude for what's not wrong or the strength you're gaining

Key points for effectiveness:

- Don't minimize real problems; focus on authentic silver linings
- Use this especially for minor annoyances to build the habit
- Share your insights with others when appropriate

Practice #5: The Gratitude Anchor

Why it's powerful: This practice turns daily activities into automatic gratitude triggers, making it a sustainable habit.

Steps:

1. Choose 3 daily activities you always do, like:
    a. Morning coffee
    b. Stopping at red lights
    c. Washing your hands
2. For each activity, select a gratitude focus:
    a. Coffee → Career opportunities
    b. Red lights → Health and safety
    c. Washing hands → Home comforts
3. Every time you perform that activity, think of one specific gratitude in that category

Key points for effectiveness:

1. Start with just one anchor, then gradually add more
2. Choose activities you do consistently
3. Keep categories broad enough for variety
4. Change the anchors if they become routine or stale

100 More Uncommon Gratitude Practices

To keep things fresh and deepen your gratitude practice, try these 97 unconventional approaches. I recommend choosing one practice for each day. The last three are left blank for you to personalize—I believe by then, you'll be inspired and capable of creating your own.

1. **Reverse Bucket List**: List all the amazing experiences you've already had instead of future desires.

2. **Gratitude Photo Walk**: Take pictures of small, easily overlooked things you're thankful for.

3. **"What If" Gratitude**: Imagine life without basic things you take for granted, like running water or air we breathe.

4. **Sensory Gratitude Meditation**: Focus on being thankful for each of your senses, one at a time.

5. **Thank-You Notes to Inanimate Objects**: Write notes of appreciation to objects you use daily.

6. **Gratitude Time Travel**: Thank your past self for good decisions or habits that have improved your life.

7. **"Hard Gratitude" Practice**: Find something to appreciate in difficult people or situations.

8. **Gratitude Mapping**: Create a web that connects all the people and events that made something possible for you.

9. **Random Acts of Thanks**: Thank people who aren't expecting it, like the bus driver or maintenance staff.

10. **Gratitude Jar for Others**: Write down what you appreciate about someone else, and give them the collection.

11. **Future Gratitude Letters**: Write a letter to your future self, thanking them for the progress you're making.

12. **Gratitude Soundscape**: Record short voice memos whenever you feel grateful throughout the day.

13. **Gratitude Math**: Calculate how many people contributed to something simple, like your morning coffee.

14. **Complaint-to-Gratitude Conversion**: Turn every complaint into an expression of appreciation.

15. **Anonymous Gratitude Drops**: Leave thank-you notes in public places for strangers to find.

16. **Gratitude Interview**: Ask others what they're grateful for and why, and document their perspectives.

17. **Gratitude Genealogy**: Trace back who taught you important skills or values, and thank them.

18. **Elements Gratitude**: Focus on one natural element (water, air, earth, fire) and express gratitude for it.

19. **Micro-Moment Appreciation**: Set random alarms to pause and find something to appreciate right at that moment.

20. **Gratitude Drawing**: Sketch simple images of things you're thankful for, even if you're not an artist.

21. **Language Gratitude**: Learn to say "thank you" in different languages, and use them regularly.

22. **Seasonal Gratitude Wheel**: Document unique things to appreciate during each season.

23. **Gratitude Time Capsule**: Write down your current gratitudes and revisit them in the future.

24. **"What Went Right" Journal**: End each day by listing things that worked out, even the smallest ones.

25. **Gratitude Rituals**: Create a personal ritual, like lighting a candle every time you express thanks, to make gratitude a sacred practice.

26. **Gratitude for Challenges**: Thank challenges in your life for the lessons they've taught you.

27. **Creative Gratitude Affirmations**: Write or speak affirmations that express your gratitude in creative, poetic ways.

28. **Gratitude Playlist**: Curate a playlist of songs that make you feel thankful or reflect on things you're grateful for.

29. **Gratitude Vision Board**: Create a vision board that represents things you're thankful for and continue to add to it.

30. **Gratitude Walks**: Take a walk with the intention of noticing everything you're grateful for in your surroundings—nature, people, the architecture, or even the sky.

31. **Gratitude at the End of a Task**: After completing a task, big or small, take a moment to express gratitude for your ability to finish it and the steps it took to get there.

32. **Gratitude Visualization**: Sit in a quiet place and vividly imagine all the things you're thankful for, seeing and feeling them as clearly as possible in your mind's eye.

33. **Gratitude Ritual Before Meals**: Before eating, take a moment to silently express gratitude for the food, the people who made it, and the nourishment it provides.

34. **Color Gratitude**: Choose a color each day, and notice all the things around you that reflect that color, feeling thankful for their presence.

35. **Gratitude for Your Body**: Focus on a specific part of your body each day and express gratitude for its function, like your legs for walking, or your eyes for seeing.

36. **Gratitude Affirmation Cards**: Write gratitude affirmations on small cards, and carry them with you to read throughout the day.

37. **Gratitude for the Unseen**: Acknowledge and be thankful for things you can't physically see but benefit from, like the air, the internet, or the community around you.

38. **Gratitude Reflection Before Bed**: Before going to sleep, reflect on everything that went well that day, no matter how small, and express your thanks for it.

39. **Gratitude in Silence**: Spend a set amount of time in complete silence, focusing only on feelings of gratitude, without words or thoughts interrupting the flow.

40. **Gratitude Gardening**: While planting or tending to your garden, express thanks for the growth, the earth, and the process of nurturing life.

41. **Gratitude for Your Limitations**: Take time to appreciate the limitations or boundaries in your life, recognizing how they help you grow, focus, and become more resourceful.

42. **Gratitude for Obstacles**: Instead of seeing obstacles as roadblocks, find what you can be grateful for in them—the lessons, personal growth, or new opportunities they bring.

43. **Gratitude for Technology**: Set aside a moment to appreciate the technology in your life, like the internet, your phone, or your computer, for the convenience and connectivity they provide.

44. **Gratitude for Unfinished Projects**: Acknowledge the unfinished tasks in your life and be grateful for what you've learned or the potential for growth that still lies within them.

45. **Gratitude for Strangers**: Randomly thank strangers in passing for no particular reason, simply acknowledging their existence and the positive energy they bring to the world.

46. **Gratitude Through Art**: Create abstract or freeform art—whether it's drawing, painting, or sculpture—expressing gratitude without any specific focus, just a flow of thankfulness.

47. **Gratitude in Motion**: While engaging in physical movement, like yoga, running, or dancing, focus on expressing gratitude for your body's ability to move, stretch, and grow.

48. **Gratitude for Sound**: Throughout the day, pause to appreciate the sounds around you, from the hum of your environment to the voices of loved ones, acknowledging the richness they bring to your life.

49. **Gratitude for Silence**: Spend time in complete silence and reflect on how the absence of noise brings peace and clarity to your life.

50. **Gratitude for Time**: Set aside moments to reflect on how precious time is, acknowledging and appreciating both the present moment and the time you've been given.

51. **Gratitude for Mistakes**: Identify and appreciate mistakes or failures in your life, acknowledging the lessons and growth they have brought you.

52. **Gratitude for Everyday Conversations**: Reflect on the meaningful connections in daily conversations, whether with family, friends, or even strangers, and express appreciation for them.

53. **Gratitude for Routine**: Focus on the simple, daily routines that keep your life stable and grounded, and express thanks for the comfort they bring.

54. **Gratitude for Emotional Growth**: Take a moment to thank yourself for emotional resilience, recognizing how challenges have helped you build emotional strength.

55. **Gratitude for Non-Material Gifts**: Reflect on the intangible gifts in life—such as love, kindness, wisdom, or laughter—and express gratitude for their presence.

56. **Gratitude for Your Mistakes in the Present**: In the middle of making a mistake, take a moment to be grateful for the lesson that's unfolding right before your eyes.

57. **Gratitude for Small Joys**: Focus on and express gratitude for the tiny, fleeting moments of joy—like a smile from a stranger or a warm cup of tea—that often go unnoticed.

58. **Gratitude for Personal Growth**: At the end of each week, reflect on your personal growth—whether emotional, physical, or intellectual—and express thanks for the progress you've made, no matter how small.

59. **Gratitude for Today's Opportunities**: Reflect each morning on the opportunities the day holds and express appreciation for the chance to make choices.

60. **Gratitude for Your Inner Strength**: Take time to acknowledge your resilience and inner strength during challenging moments, expressing gratitude for your capacity to endure.

61. **Gratitude for the Present Moment**: Practice mindfulness and express gratitude for the here and now, appreciating the moment without focusing on past or future concerns.

62. **Gratitude for Your Support System**: Identify and thank those who support you, whether family, friends, colleagues, or mentors, for being there when needed.

63. **Gratitude for Your Failures**: Take a moment to recognize failures as stepping stones and express gratitude for the lessons they've taught you.

64. **Gratitude for Your Future Self**: Reflect on your future accomplishments and express gratitude for the person you will become through the choices you make today.

65. **Gratitude for New Experiences**: When encountering something new, whether it's a place, activity, or person, express thanks for the opportunity to grow and expand your horizons.

66. **Gratitude for Patience**: Appreciate the moments when patience is required, recognizing how those times help you grow and develop emotional resilience.

67. **Gratitude for Everyday Comforts**: Acknowledge the comfort in your daily life—like a warm blanket, a favorite chair, or a soothing shower—and express appreciation for them.

68. **Gratitude for Random Acts of Kindness**: Reflect on random acts of kindness from others and express thanks for the way they brighten your day.

69. **Gratitude for the Breath**: Take moments throughout the day to pause, breathe deeply, and express gratitude for your ability to breathe and experience life.

70. **Gratitude for Your Surroundings**: Appreciate the physical space around you—whether your home, office, or nature—and reflect on how it supports and nourishes you.

71. **Gratitude for Your Work**: Express appreciation for the work you do, whether for a living or for personal fulfillment, acknowledging its value in your life.

72. **Gratitude for the People You Don't Know Yet**: Be grateful for the people you will meet in the future, appreciating the potential for new relationships and experiences they bring.

73. **Gratitude for Your Body's Wisdom**: Acknowledge and thank your body for its ability to heal, adapt, and communicate through physical sensations.

74. **Gratitude for Nature's Cycles**: Reflect on the cyclical nature of life, such as seasons, birth, growth, and decay, and express gratitude for the rhythm they bring.

75. **Gratitude for Your Senses**: Each day, focus on one sense (sight, hearing, touch, smell, taste) and express thanks for how it enriches your experience of the world.

76. **Gratitude for the Ordinary**: Recognize and appreciate the beauty and value in everyday activities like doing the dishes or walking to work.

77. **Gratitude for Unpredictability**: Embrace the unpredictable nature of life and express gratitude for the surprises and spontaneity it brings.

78. **Gratitude for Your Mind**: Appreciate the way your mind works, whether it's solving problems, imagining, or simply processing the world around you.

79. **Gratitude for Music**: Reflect on the joy and emotional connection that music brings to your life and express gratitude for your favorite songs or artists.

80. **Gratitude for Technology's Impact**: Take a moment to appreciate the convenience and connection technology has brought into your life, such as access to information and communication.

81. **Gratitude for Movement**: Reflect on and express gratitude for the ability to move—whether through exercise, walking, or dancing—and the freedom it provides.

82. **Gratitude for Quiet Moments**: Appreciate the rare and peaceful moments of silence, when you can reconnect with your inner self.

83. **Gratitude for Your Emotions**: Acknowledge the full range of your emotions—joy, sorrow, anger, fear—and express thanks for their role in making you human.

84. **Gratitude for Creativity**: Recognize the creative energy within you, whether through art, problem-solving, or expression, and give thanks for its flow.

85. **Gratitude for the Space to Rest**: Acknowledge the importance of rest and relaxation, and express gratitude for the opportunity to restore your energy.

86. **Gratitude for Challenges**: Thank the challenges in your life for the wisdom and growth they have provided.

87. **Gratitude for Time Alone**: Reflect on the peace and clarity that comes from time spent alone and express gratitude for the solitude that helps you recharge.

88. **Gratitude for Serendipity**: Appreciate the times when life's unplanned moments lead to pleasant surprises or opportunities you didn't expect.

89. **Gratitude for Your Journey**: Reflect on the path that has led you to where you are today, expressing thanks for the experiences that shaped you.

90. **Gratitude for Acts of Self-Love**: Acknowledge moments when you practice self-care, self-compassion, or self-respect, and be grateful for honoring yourself.

91. **Gratitude for Wisdom from Others**: Appreciate the guidance and wisdom from mentors, family, friends, or even strangers, and thank them for their contributions to your life.

92. **Gratitude for Small Wins**: Celebrate even the smallest accomplishments in your day, whether it's finishing a task or just making progress.

93. **Gratitude for Being Alive**: At any given moment, express thanks for the fact that you are alive to experience the world.

94. **Gratitude for Your Imagination**: Appreciate your imagination for its ability to help you visualize, create, and dream.

95. **Gratitude for Laughter**: Acknowledge moments of humor and laughter, whether with others or alone, and express gratitude for its joy and release.

96. **Gratitude for the Moon and Stars**: Spend a moment in awe of the night sky, expressing gratitude for the beauty and constancy of the celestial world.

97. **Gratitude for Your Connections with Others**: Reflect on the relationships in your life, whether deep or fleeting, and express thanks for the human connections that enrich your experience.

98.   < Your New Practice No.1 >

99.   < Your New Practice No.2 >

100.   < Your New Practice No.3 >

General Implementation Tips for Routines

1. Start with just one practice and focus on consistency
2. Do it for 21 days before adding another practice
3. Track your progress with a simple journal or app
4. Share your experience with a friend to stay accountable
5. Focus on feeling gratitude, not just going through the emotions
6. Notice changes in your mood, relationships, and overall well-being

Gratitude Rituals

Life can be divided into two types of experiences: the routine events that shape our daily lives and the special occasions that stand out as key memories. Habits guide us through the routines, creating a rhythm to our existence. But special occasions—whether it's delivering a presentation, reconnecting with a long-lost friend, or attending a once-in-a-lifetime event—carry an emotional weight that lingers far beyond the moment itself. These moments often become defining memories, leaving an "aftertaste" that can either empower or hinder us as we move forward in life.

To ensure these key moments leave us feeling inspired and uplifted, we need to approach them with intention and purpose. This is where Gratitude Rituals come into play. Gratitude Rituals are not necessarily tied to religious practices, though they can be. Instead, they are deeply spiritual—they connect us to our higher selves, the best versions of who we can be. Spirituality, in this sense, is the essence of growth, empowerment, and inspiration—the "spirit" within us that fuels transformation.

I've developed a framework for creating meaningful Gratitude Rituals that will help you harness gratitude as a powerful tool during these significant moments. This framework is designed to shift your energy and perspective, empowering you to approach key events with positivity and grace. By integrating gratitude into these special occasions, you can turn them into transformative memories that fuel your journey and elevate your life. Let gratitude be the guide that helps you embrace these extraordinary moments with confidence, joy, and purpose.

The G.R.A.T.E.R. Framework for Gratitude Rituals

1. **G**round Yourself
   a. Create a sacred space or moment of stillness before the event
   b. Practice deep breathing
   c. Set a clear intention to approach the occasion with an open heart and grateful mindset

2. **R**eflect and Recall
   a. Before the event, spend 5-10 minutes journaling about:
      i. Past moments of joy related to this type of occasion
      ii. People who have supported you in reaching this moment
      iii. Personal growth and challenges you've overcome
   b. Create a mental movie of positive memories and emotions

3. **A**cknowledge the Layers
   a. Identify multiple levels of gratitude:
      - Physical (health, comfort, basic needs)
      - Emotional (relationships, support, love)
      - Spiritual (personal growth, universal connection)
      - Potential (opportunities, possibilities)
   b. Write down 3-5 specific things you're grateful for in each layer

4. **T**ouch Points of Gratitude
   a. Create physical or sensory anchors for gratitude:
      - A special piece of jewelry
      - A meaningful object in your pocket

○ A specific scent or essential oil
        ○ A written gratitude note to yourself
- These touch points serve as reminders and reset mechanisms during the event

5. **Energetic Preparation**
   a. Visualization meditation (10-15 minutes before the event)
      a. Imagine yourself surrounded by a golden light of appreciation
      b. See yourself moving through the event with grace, openness, and joy
      c. Feel the vibration of gratitude resonating through your body
   b. Use positive affirmations like:
      a. "I am open to the abundance of this moment"
      b. "Gratitude flows through me effortlessly"
      c. "I choose to see the beauty in this experience"

6. **Ritualistic Moments**
   a. Create specific ritual points during the event:
      i. Pause and take 3 conscious breaths
      ii. Silently acknowledge one thing you're grateful for
      iii. Make eye contact and mentally thank someone
      iv. Write a quick gratitude note if appropriate

Extend and Reflect

The micro-rituals keep you connected to your grateful state. After the event, take time to reflect on the experience by journaling and noting unexpected moments of joy or connection. Show appreciation by sending thank-you messages to those involved and perform a gratitude meditation to deepen your positive emotions. This practice helps to integrate the experience fully, reinforcing the positive emotional state and leaving you with a sense of fulfillment and connection.

Customization Tips:

- Adapt the framework to suit different occasions (weddings, graduations, career milestones, personal celebrations)
- Choose rituals that feel authentic and meaningful to you
- Practice regularly to make gratitude a natural state

Practice Progression:

- Start with smaller occasions to build your gratitude muscle
- Be patient with yourself
- Understand that some days will feel easier than others

Gratitude Meditation

Meditation, at its core, is the practice of intentionally training the mind to achieve a state of focused awareness or calm clarity. Your understanding aligns with many teachings: meditation involves quieting the "monkey mind"—that restless, scattered stream of thoughts that can keep us perpetually distracted. Through meditation, we aim to shift from this reactive state to one of intentional focus, where the mind becomes a tool we control, not a force that controls us.

Why Meditate?

Meditation is a lifeline in today's overstimulated world, where our minds often race with countless thoughts, worries, and distractions. When we meditate, we give ourselves the chance to pause, reset, and gain clarity. Rather than drowning in a flood of unhelpful thoughts, meditation allows us to focus our mental energy on what truly matters—whether that's achieving a goal, feeling more present, or finding inner peace. This clarity and intentionality can improve our emotional well-being, enhance our focus, and unlock creativity and resilience.

How to Meditate?

As you might have noticed, there is no single "correct" way to meditate. Meditation practices come in many forms, from mindfulness and breathing exercises to guided visualizations, mantra-based techniques, and movement-based approaches like yoga or tai chi. While methods may differ, the goal remains the same: to quiet the mind and cultivate awareness and eventually mindfulness.

The Basic Mechanism of Meditation

According to my understanding, the thoughts that overwhelm us into a state of self-induced paralysis are deeply intertwined with our breathing. When a person feels tense or anxious, their thoughts often race uncontrollably, creating a whirlwind of mental noise. This mental chaos manifests physically in their breath—rapid, shallow, and irregular. On the other hand, a relaxed person experiences slower, more balanced thoughts, reflected in deep, calm, and rhythmic breathing.

This intrinsic connection between the mind and breath reveals a powerful truth: the gateway to stillness and mindfulness begins with mastering our breath. By consciously observing and regulating our breathing, we can steady our racing thoughts, center ourselves, and create the inner space necessary for meditation.

<u>**Meditation entails the following key phases:**</u>

Awareness of the Present Moment: Meditation begins by anchoring your awareness to something in the present—such as your breath, a mantra, or the sensations in your body. This focus helps quiet the mental noise.

Acknowledging and Letting Go: As thoughts inevitably arise, the practice involves noticing them without judgment and gently redirecting your focus back to your anchor. This process trains your mind to respond calmly to distractions.

Sustained Focus: Over time, with practice, you build the ability to sustain focus for longer periods. This allows you to access deeper states of calm and clarity.

In exploring the transformative power of this practice, I have gathered insights from some of the most highly regarded and best-selling books on meditation and mindfulness. These books offer profound wisdom and practical tools for cultivating a meaningful meditation practice. They include "The Miracle of Mindfulness" by Thich Nhat Hanh, "Breath: The New Science of a Lost Art" by James Nestor, ."Mindfulness: An Eight-Week Plan for Finding Peace in a Frantic World" by Mark Williams and Danny Penman, "The Power of Now" by Eckhart Tolle and "The Untethered Soul: The Journey Beyond Yourself" by Michael A. Singer

The insights gathered from these books will help you fine-tune your meditation practice to suit your needs

Anchor Gratitude in the Present Moment

Gratitude is most powerful when focused on the present moment. By appreciating life's gifts in the "now," you deepen your connection to gratitude and enhance its impact.

Actionable Tip: Before starting, repeat: "Right now, I am grateful for..." to center your focus on the current moment.

Combine Gratitude with Deep Breathing

Pairing gratitude with slow, intentional breathing helps create a calm, receptive mental state. Synchronize your thoughts of gratitude with each breath for greater emotional resonance.

Actionable Tip: Practice the 4-7-8 breathing technique while visualizing something or someone you are thankful for.

Make Gratitude a Daily Habit

Consistency is key to making gratitude a transformative force in your life. By linking gratitude meditation to an existing daily habit, you can build a sustainable practice.

Actionable Tip: Use reminders, such as a sticky note or alarm, to set aside a consistent time each day for gratitude meditation.

Visualize Gratitude for Emotional Impact

Visualization enhances the emotional depth of gratitude, making it more vivid and meaningful. Picture specific moments, people, or experiences that you are deeply thankful for.

Actionable Tip: Visualize each point of gratitude as a growing light within you, expanding with each breath and filling you with warmth.

Release Judgment and Redirect Focus

Distractions are natural during meditation. Instead of resisting them, acknowledge them with kindness and gently guide your focus back to gratitude.

Actionable Tip: When distracted, say: "I see you, but I choose gratitude," and return to your chosen point of focus.

Which Meditation is the Best ?

The beauty of meditation lies in its flexibility. You are free to experiment and find a technique that resonates with you and aligns with your goals. Whether you prefer a structured guided meditation or simply sitting in silence to observe your breath, the key is to prioritize consistency. The state of a quiet, focused mind is the ultimate destination, no matter which path you take.

This approach encourages an open mindset, empowering you to tailor meditation to your unique needs while still harnessing its transformative benefits.

Gratitude Retreat

If meditation is the daily practice of quieting the mind and attuning to joy, then a retreat is an opportunity to step back from life's chaos and fully immerse yourself in rejuvenation. A retreat allows us to temporarily distance ourselves from external distractions and reestablish our connection with our original state—a state of peace, clarity, and alignment with our true selves.

Interestingly, the word "retreat" can sometimes carry a negative connotation, as if it implies running away from a battle. But what if we saw it differently? Rather than a withdrawal, a retreat can be viewed as a restart or a reboot. Much like how restarting a computer clears out glitches and restores optimal performance, a retreat gives us the space to recalibrate, replenish, and return to life with renewed strength and purpose.

When approached with intention, a retreat becomes a powerful way to align the mind, body, and soul, helping us shed accumulated stress and rediscover our inner balance. It is not about escaping life but rather returning to it—recharged, refreshed, and ready to embrace it fully.

The 3R Framework for a successful Gratitude Retreat

A Gratitude Retreat can be structured around a unique 3R Framework designed to nurture your Mind, Body, and Athma through intentional practices that align with the processes of Reflection, Replenishment, and Reignition. This framework provides a simple yet transformative path to create a retreat that fosters deep gratitude and renewal.

1. REFLECT: Ground Yourself in Gratitude

Purpose: Begin by quieting the noise of daily life and reflecting on what you are grateful for. This step helps center your focus and set the tone for the retreat.

Activities:

- **Gratitude Journaling:** Spend time writing about the people, experiences, and opportunities you are thankful for. Use prompts like "What made me smile recently?" or "What challenges have taught me valuable lessons?"
- **Meditative Reflection:** Practice gratitude-based meditation. Sit in stillness and visualize moments that brought you joy or peace.

- **Nature Connection:** Walk mindfully in nature, observing its beauty, and express silent thanks for its gifts.

2. REPLENISH: Nourish Mind, Body, and Soul

Purpose: This phase focuses on activities that replenish your energy and align your inner and outer well-being.

Activities:

- **Mind:** Engage in calming practices like guided visualization or breathwork to clear mental clutter and create space for positive thoughts.
- **Body:** Prioritize nurturing physical activities like yoga, stretching, or simply enjoying a balanced, nourishing meal with gratitude for the food and its source.
- **Athma (Soul):** Take time for soul-enriching practices, such as reading inspiring literature, writing a gratitude letter to someone, or engaging in a creative activity that brings joy.

3. REIGNITE: Create Intentions for the Future

Purpose: Use the final phase of the retreat to reignite your passions and set intentions to carry the gratitude mindset forward.

Activities:

1. Future Visioning: Write down how you want gratitude to shape your life moving forward. What habits or practices will you commit to when you return to daily life?

2. Gratitude Rituals: Develop a gratitude ritual, such as saying a gratitude mantra each morning or ending the day with a reflection on one thing you appreciated.

3. Sharing Gratitude: Before concluding your retreat, share your gratitude with others. This could be through a heartfelt message, a call to someone you love, or a simple act of kindness.

Practical Tips for Implementing the 3R Framework

Setting the Space: Whether at home or in a chosen retreat location, create an environment that feels peaceful and distraction-free. Use soothing music, candles, or natural elements to enhance the experience.

Time Commitment: Your retreat can be as short as a few hours or span several days. Choose a structure that fits your lifestyle and allows for depth without stress.

Journaling: Keep a dedicated gratitude retreat journal to document insights, emotions, and intentions throughout the process.

"No Device" policy: To make your retreat profoundly impactful, adopt a No Device Policy. Disconnecting from all devices—phones, tablets, laptops, or anything else demanding your attention—will allow you to fully immerse yourself in the present moment. Remember, this retreat is about dedicating 100% of your attention to the most important person in your life: *you.*

By setting aside distractions, you create the space to reconnect with the most wonderful gift life has given you: Gratitude. Devices often tether us to the noise of the outside world, but during your retreat, the focus should shift inward—to your thoughts, feelings, and the deeper sense of connection within.

Commit to this policy as an act of self-love, and allow yourself the freedom to rediscover peace, clarity, and the joy of being fully present.

By following the 3R Framework, your Gratitude Retreat becomes more than just a pause—it becomes a powerful reboot for your mind, body, and athma. It creates a lasting impact, helping you sustain gratitude as a transformative force in your life. Let this retreat not just rejuvenate you but inspire you to live with gratitude every single day.

IF EVERYTHING AROUND SEEMS DARK, LOOK AGAIN,

YOU MAY BE THE LIGHT

RUMI

Potential Challenges & Solutions

The journey to making gratitude a consistent part of your life is not without its challenges. However, here are some practical workarounds to overcome common hurdles you may encounter along the way.

If you're feeling stressed, take a deep breath and remember this: your breath is the original anti-stress app, and it doesn't even need Wi-Fi. Close your eyes (unless you're driving!) and focus entirely on your breath—the cool, crisp inhale, the tiny pause that's like your lungs saying, "Hold up, let's savor this moment," and the soothing exhale that feels like your body giving a dramatic sigh of relief.

Feel the air waltzing into your nostrils, filling your lungs, and then swaying out like it just had a peaceful retreat. Notice your chest rising and falling—it's your body's way of reminding you that, hey, it's still on your side. With every breath, let go of tension like you're tossing out last year's bad resolutions.

This isn't just breathing; it's stress eviction. Every exhale kicks out a little more worry, leaving room for clarity, calm, and maybe even a sprinkle of hope. Who knew the simple act of inhaling and exhaling could turn you into a zen ninja?

If negativity creeps in, don't wrestle with it—acknowledge it, like a toddler throwing a tantrum, and then gently shift your focus to gratitude. Think of it like changing the channel from a boring infomercial to your favorite feel-good show. Maybe it's the warmth of the sun on your face, a random smile from a stranger, or just the fact that your Wi-Fi didn't drop during a crucial moment. These tiny gratitude nuggets are your mental anchors, gently pulling you back to the brighter side of life.

With each moment of appreciation, you're essentially telling negativity, "Thanks for stopping by, but I'm all set." And just like that, you're inviting peace, perspective, and maybe even a little joy to crash the party. Gratitude: the ultimate negativity bouncer.

If you're feeling overwhelmed, ditch the bells and whistles i.e. simplify your ritual. Strip your ritual down to its basics. Forget perfection; the essence is what matters. Take a moment to breathe deeply, say a simple affirmation, or just acknowledge one thing you're grateful for (like surviving another day without spilling coffee on yourself).

Do it with love—love for the moment, love for the process, and let's be honest, love for not adding more to your already overflowing plate. By focusing on the heart of the ritual, you'll trade chaos for calm and come out the other side feeling like a zen ninja, ready to conquer whatever comes next.

If affirmations are being met with resistance, try a little sneaky mental judo with lofty, empowering questions instead. So, instead of declaring, "I am open to the abundance of this moment" (and hearing your inner skeptic mutter, "Yeah, right…"), reframe it as, "Why am I so open to the abundance of this moment?" See what happens? Your mind—ever the nosy detective—starts hunting for reasons this could be true.

This clever trick bypasses your inner critic and shifts your mindset from "Nope" to "Hmm, maybe!" It's like giving your subconscious a mystery to solve, and who doesn't love solving a good mystery? By focusing on curiosity and discovery, you turn your mental roadblock into a springboard for possibility. Suddenly, inviting positive energy feels less like convincing yourself and more like uncovering a hidden truth. How's that for a plot twist?

Remember, the goal isn't to win an imaginary gold medal for flawless mindfulness—it's about simply showing up, messy thoughts and all. Each time you practice, it's like giving your brain a little nudge toward becoming a gratitude-seeking missile. Slowly but surely, you're rewiring yourself to default to appreciation and joy. Progress, not perfection, my friend—after all, even Picasso probably spilled a little paint once upon a time.

Technology & Gratitude

Technology, when wielded mindfully, becomes a transformative tool for cultivating gratitude. In our hyper-connected world, digital platforms can either fragment our attention or deepen our capacity for appreciation. Properly used, technology can create intentional spaces for reflection, providing personalized prompts, tracking emotional growth, and connecting us with supportive communities. Smart notifications and AI-driven coaching can gently guide us towards recognizing life's subtle blessings. The key is conscious engagement—using digital tools as supportive companions in our gratitude journey, not as distractions. By setting clear boundaries, selecting purpose-driven applications, and maintaining human-centered interactions, we can harness technology's potential to amplify mindfulness, foster emotional intelligence, and nurture a profound sense of thankfulness.

Block Digital Distractions

Modern technology floods us with notifications, depleting our mental energy and stealing moments of reflection. The key is strategic digital management:

1. **Screen Time Limitations**
   - Use built-in phone features to set daily app limits
   - Create "no-tech" zones in your home
   - Designate specific times for digital disconnection

2. **Distraction Blocking Tools**
   - Apps like Forest, Freedom, and RescueTime
   - Block social media during focused periods
   - Create intentional digital boundaries

Gratitude Technology Toolkit

1. **Pomodoro with Gratitude Intervals**
   - Use 25-minute work sprints
   - Insert 5-minute gratitude reflection between sessions
   - Recommended apps: Focus To-Do, Be Focused

2. **Smart Gratitude Reminders**
   - Set daily prompts at meaningful times
   - Use apps like Presently, Gratitude, ThinkUp
   - Customize notifications to feel personal, not intrusive

AI-Powered Introspection

Use AI tools like ChatGPT and Claude to generate deep reflection questions. One advantage of "chatting" with AI over chatting with a normal person is that AI doesn't feel tired, doesn't need to take breaks, and most importantly, won't get angry if you ask questions you feel are too simple.

SAMPLE AI PROMPTS FOR GRATITUDE

↳ Act as an Expert Clarity Coach. I want to **gain clarity on a situation I'm facing.** The situation is [describe your situation]. Please generate specific and thought-provoking questions that will help me understand my emotions, identify key factors, explore options, and move forward effectively.

↳ Act as an Expert Personal Development Coach. Your role is to **guide me towards clarity** by asking thoughtful and probing follow-up questions based solely on my responses. Do not provide answers or suggestions—only ask questions that help me explore my thoughts, feelings, and options further. I will type 'END SESSION' when I feel I have achieved the clarity I need. Let's begin.

Note: Clearly understanding what you want is a crucial skill to develop for making AI the perfect tool. This ability will also help you master the art of asking insightful questions—an essential key to growth.

Digital Gratitude Enhancement

The journey of integrating technology into your gratitude practice begins with a comprehensive digital wellness audit. This process requires deep self-reflection and honest assessment of your current technological interactions. Start by mapping out your daily digital landscape, examining how your devices and applications currently influence your mental and emotional state. Look closely at the frequency of notifications, the types of content consuming your attention, and moments where digital interactions potentially disrupt your inner peace.

During this audit, identify specific opportunities where technology can be transformed from a distraction into a supportive tool for gratitude cultivation. This might involve recognizing patterns of mindless scrolling, understanding trigger points for digital overwhelm, and discovering potential moments for meaningful reflection. The goal is to design a personalized intervention plan that aligns with your unique lifestyle and emotional needs.

Habit building becomes the next critical phase of this technological gratitude transformation. Begin with modest, achievable goals—dedicating just five minutes daily to intentional gratitude practices facilitated by carefully selected digital tools. These initial moments should feel gentle and unintimidating, creating a sustainable entry point into a more mindful digital experience. As comfort grows, gradually expand your engagement, introducing more nuanced reflection techniques and longer practice durations.

Tracking progress becomes essential in maintaining motivation. Utilize digital journaling apps or gratitude-specific platforms that allow you to document your journey, providing visual representations of your growing practice. Celebrate small victories, whether it's consistently using a gratitude app for a week or noticing subtle shifts in your emotional landscape.

When selecting technology to support your gratitude practice, adopt a discerning approach. Prioritize applications and tools that offer minimal notifications to prevent digital overwhelm. The ideal platform should feature an intuitive, user-friendly interface that feels natural and unobtrusive. Privacy considerations are paramount—choose solutions that respect your data and emotional vulnerabilities.

Customization emerges as a crucial criterion. The most effective gratitude technologies will allow personalization, enabling you to tailor prompts, reflection times, and interaction styles to your specific preferences. This adaptability ensures that the technology genuinely serves your personal growth rather than forcing you into a predetermined framework.

By approaching digital gratitude enhancement through this strategic, mindful lens, technology transforms from a potential source of distraction into a powerful ally in your journey of appreciation and self-discovery. The key lies not in wholesale rejection of digital tools, but in consciously reshaping their role in our emotional and spiritual development.

Key Takeaway

Technology isn't the enemy of gratitude—it's a powerful ally when used mindfully. The goal is creating a digital ecosystem that nurtures reflection, appreciation, and personal growth.

Next Steps

As we reach the final pages of this book, I want you to pause. Take a deep breath. This isn't just another conclusion—it's the beginning of your most important journey.

I remember a moment that changed everything for me. Years ago, sitting in the depths of my own darkness, surrounded by failures and heartbreaks, I would have laughed at the idea that gratitude could be a life-changing force. Concepts, theories, and motivational speeches are like beautiful maps—but they remain useless unless you actually start walking.

The most revolutionary book in the world cannot transform your life. The most inspiring speaker cannot change your reality. The most profound concept remains just that—a concept—until you decide to take that first step.

Gratitude is not a destination. It's not a finish line you cross. It's a daily choice. It's a muscle you build. It's a lens through which you choose to see the world.

Right now, at this very moment, you have a choice. You can close this book and let these words become just another forgotten inspiration. Or you can make a commitment—to yourself, to your potential, to the life waiting to unfold before you.

Your First Mission

Before you put this book down, I challenge you to do three things:

1. **Grow back your Inner Child***

2. **Write Down Your Gratitude Commitment**
   - Take a blank page
   - Write:
     "I Commit to practicing Gratitude as the way of Life"
   - Sign and date it
   - This is your personal contract with possibility

3. **Identify Your Starting Point**
   - What's one area of your life that feels stuck?
   - How can gratitude be your first step in transforming that area?
   - Write down a specific, actionable gratitude practice for this area

4. **Design Your Life of Gratitude**
   - Use the Gratitude Triad
   - Use the tools and techniques mentioned in this book
   - Create practices that suit you to live fully in gratitude
   - and … ACT ON IT!

Remember, transformation isn't about perfection. It's about progress. Some days, gratitude will flow easily. Some days, it will feel like climbing a mountain. Both are part of the journey.

The life you've been dreaming of—the one filled with joy, purpose, and abundance—it's not waiting for you somewhere in the future. It's waiting for you to recognize it right now.

GRATITUDE IS THE KEY. ACTION IS THE TURN OF THAT KEY.

The world doesn't need another person who understands gratitude intellectually. The world needs people who live gratitude courageously, authentically, and transformatively.

Are you ready?

Your supercharged life starts now.

Not tomorrow. Not next week. Right. This. Moment.

There's a child in all of us. Once upon a time, that child was alive and kicking, marveling at the world with wide-eyed wonder. Back then, almost everything made us go, "Wow!"—a butterfly, a rainbow, or even just the way a flashlight could turn a dark room into a stage for shadow puppets. Everything was a Miracle.

But then adulthood happened. We "grew up," not necessarily because we wanted to but because society handed us a checklist titled How to Be an Adult™ : Shoulds and Should Nots—and just like that, the things that made us say "Wow" dwindled to a handful. Now, we chase that feeling in other ways—like magic shows, where we knowingly get tricked but still lean forward in amazement, because deep down, we miss that wow.

Here's the thing: the inner child in us hasn't gone anywhere. It's still there—sassy, curious, and ready to remind us what truly matters. That inner child is a superhero in disguise: it's fearless, imaginative, and full of possibilities, unburdened by the self-imposed limits we pick up as adults. Reconnecting with that child is the secret to a supercharged life.

Take relationships, for example. When we argue with someone we love, just to prove we're right, our inner child is practically jumping up and down, waving a red flag, screaming, "STOP! You're winning the argument but losing the connection!" It knows the cost of pride better than we do. Or when your son forgets his lunch box and instead of asking if he was hungry or tired, you greet him with a scolding. Your inner child whispers (or shouts, depending on its mood), "What you really want to say is 'I was worried about you.' Say that instead!"

The trick isn't to "grow up" but to grow back—back to that child who knew how to marvel, how to connect, and how to let love and curiosity lead the way. Listen to your inner child. It's smarter than you think and way better at making shadow puppets.

The key to getting Supercharged and living Supercharged is to keep that inner child alive, vibrant, and unapologetically playful.. How does that inner child go from a bright spark to a flickering light? The same way any lively, enthusiastic kid turns gloomy and withdrawn—lack of attention and love. A child thrives when you listen to it with curiosity, love, and amazement. It gets inspired when you let it play, explore, and dream wildly.

The problem arises when we start ignoring our inner child, telling it to hush up because we have more important things to focus on which we think the child won't understand—like taxes, deadlines, or pretending we actually enjoy kale smoothies. Worse, we sometimes shun the inner child entirely because its whimsical, carefree behavior doesn't align with what society taught us is "proper" or "grown-up."

Here's the deal, though: when you ignore your inner child, you don't just lose a bit of whimsy—you lose the very essence of creativity, joy, and the kind of fearless energy that makes life an adventure. The trick isn't to outgrow that child; it's to let it grow with you. So, take that doodling break, laugh at the lamest puns, or wear mismatched socks just because they make you happy.

Life's too short to bench your inner kid—it's the part of you that makes the ride worthwhile!

Epilogue

A GLOBAL GRATITUDE REVOLUTION

We stand at the precipice of a global transformation.

Imagine a world where gratitude isn't just a personal practice, but a collective consciousness. A world where every human being recognizes their interconnectedness, where compassion flows as naturally as breath, where abundance replaces scarcity, and hope conquers fear.

This is not a utopian dream. This is a possibility waiting to be awakened.

You are not just reading a book. You are holding a blueprint for a worldwide revolution.

Every time you choose gratitude, you're not just changing your life. You're sending out a ripple that can transform generations. You become a beacon—illuminating the path for others to see the extraordinary power of appreciating life's gifts.

Think of gratitude as a viral positive infection. Each "thank you" is a seed. Each moment of appreciation is a spark. And when these sparks connect, they create a wildfire of transformation that can sweep across continents: The Gratitude Domino Effect

Imagine:

- A child learning to see abundance instead of lack
- A community that supports instead of competes
- A workplace driven by appreciation rather than fear
- A society that values connection over consumption

This is not idealism. This is the potential that lives within gratitude where your personal practice becomes a global movement. Your inner transformation becomes a catalyst for collective healing.

YOUR ROLE IN THE GLOBAL GRATITUDE MOVEMENT

You are now a Gratitude Ambassador. Your mission is not just personal growth, but planetary awakening.

- Start with Yourself: Become a living embodiment of gratitude
- Spread the Wisdom: Share, not preach
- Create Ripples: Every grateful action touches countless lives
- Be Persistent: Cultural shifts happen one heart at a time

A Collective Vision

We are not just changing individual lives. We are reimagining human potential.

Gratitude is the language of hope.

Gratitude is the currency of connection.

Gratitude is our pathway to a more conscious, compassionate world.

This book is your invitation. Not just to transform, but to be a transformer.

Are you Ready to lead the Gratitude Revolution?

The New World is waiting.

YOUR GRATITUDE, OUR COLLECTIVE FUTURE

References

1. Bono, G., Emmons, R. A. & McCullough, M. E., 2013. Gratitude and well-being: A review and theoretical integration. *Clinical Psychology Review*, 30(7), pp. 890-905.

2. Brooks, D. (2023). *How to Know a Person*. Random House.

3. Chapman, G.D. (2015). The 5 Love Languages. Chicago: Northfield Pub.

4. Clear, J. (2018). *Atomic Habits: An Easy & Proven Way to Build Good Habits & Break Bad Ones*. New York: Penguin Publishing Group.

5. Emmons, R. A. & McCullough, M. E., 2003. Counting blessings versus burdens: An experimental investigation of gratitude and subjective well-being in daily life. *Journal of Personality and Social Psychology*, 84(2), pp. 377-389.

6. Fogg, B.J. (2020). *TINY HABITS: The small changes that change everything*. S.L.: Houghton Mifflin Harcourt.

7. Gary Douglas (2012). *How Does It Get Any Better Than This? Access Consciousness Tool with Gary Douglas*. [online] YouTube. Available at: https://www.youtube.com/watch?v=_CP_f5o_seM [Accessed 4 Dec. 2024].

8. Henriette Anne Klauser (2012). *Write It Down, Make It Happen*. Simon and Schuster.

9. Jackowska, M. et al., 2015. The impact of a brief gratitude intervention on subjective well-being, biology, and emotional responses. *Journal of Positive Psychology*, 10(4), pp. 326-336.

10. Jans-Beken, L.G. and Wong, P.T., 2023. The effect of gratitude interventions on well-being: A meta-analysis. *Frontiers in Psychology*, 14, p.1130265.

11. Koo, M. et al., 2008. Beyond life satisfaction: A positive psychology approach to quality of life. *Journal of Happiness Studies*, 9(3), pp. 411-432.

12. Mcgonigal, J. (2016). Superbetter : how a gameful life can make you stronger, happier, braver and more resilient. London: Harperthorsons.

13. Sinek, S. (2009). *Start with why: How great leaders inspire everyone to take action.* London: Portfolio/Penguin.

14. Smith, J., 2022. *The Science of Gratitude. Mindful.* Available at: https://www.mindful.org/the-science-of-gratitude/ [Accessed 27 October 2024].

15. Wong, J., Brown, J. and Holman, E.A., 2018. *How Gratitude Changes You and Your Brain. Greater Good Magazine.* Available at: https://greatergood.berkeley.edu/article/item/how_gratitude_changes_you_and_your_brain [Accessed 27 October 2024].

16. Zak, P. J., 2011. The physiology of moral sentiments. *Journal of Economic Behavior & Organization*, 77(2), pp. 53-65.

About the Author

Hijaz Salahudeen is an educator, mentor, and life coach passionate about empowering individuals to embrace the transformative power of gratitude.

Believing that "Everything is a Miracle" and "Everyone is a Superhero," Hijaz promotes gratitude as a practical, life-changing tool to unlock limitless potential. Through his conversational and witty writing, he inspires readers to find the extraordinary in the ordinary and transform their perspective on life.

As a Happiness Strategist, Hijaz crafts actionable strategies to help individuals and organizations unlock their happiest selves. He emphasizes living with intention, integrity, and purpose while leaving a legacy of empowerment and hope—though always with a playful approach to happiness. With a background in engineering and management, along with nearly a decade of experience in management consulting, Hijaz has spent over six years helping leaders and organizations gain clarity and take charge of their lives.

A passionate technology enthusiast, Hijaz is dedicated to the ethical and responsible use of AI. He advocates for harnessing AI not just as a tool but as a catalyst for positive change, promoting its responsible integration into society.

Hijaz is committed to helping others live fulfilling lives rooted in gratitude, purpose, and innovation.

He can be reached at Hijaz.Here@Yahoo.Com.

Notes:

www.ingramcontent.com/pod-product-compliance
Lightning Source LLC
Chambersburg PA
CBHW060533160726
47991CB00001B/307